HIRED

The Art of Finding and Recruiting Talent

· ·

PARUL SHARMA

An imprint of
Srishti Publishers & Distributors

Srishti Publishers & Distributors
A unit of AJR Publishing LLP
212A, Peacock Lane
Shahpur Jat, New Delhi – 110 049

editorial@srishtipublishers.com

First Published by Bold,
an imprint of Srishti Publishers & Distributors in 2024

10 9 8 7 6 5 4 3 2 1

For my father, Dr Arvind Kumar Sharma, whose teachings have brought me one step closer to achieving my dreams and motivated me to write this book.

And for Yogesh, my husband, whose unconditional support has helped me throughout my writing journey.

CONTENTS

INTRODUCTION

To begin with, I would like to extend my congratulations to all readers who have chosen to read my book with the intention of gaining a fresh perspective on sourcing, talent attraction, and the recruitment process. This book is intended for aspiring professionals who seek to learn the ins and outs of recruitment, or those who are interested in pursuing it as a career.

This book is a comprehensive guide that will guide you through each stage of the recruitment process, explaining them through practical, everyday examples. Through this book, I hope to shed light on the ways in which recruitment can transform not only your own life, but the lives of others as well.

As a recruiter, I have encountered many individuals who are unaware of the true scope and impact of the profession. By connecting job seekers with meaningful opportunities, recruiters not only contribute to the success of their organizations but also add value to the lives of others. Over time, I have come to realize that recruitment provides countless opportunities to connect with the best and brightest individuals from around the world, opening doors to new perspectives and valuable experiences.

Interestingly, this book will also show you that recruitment or talent acquisition is not only meant to be mastered by recruiters but it can be learned by everyone who has an interest in changing lives and making an impact by mentoring others in their career move.

At the end of every chapter, I have provided a checklist and some exercises and questions for self-assessment for you to review and answer to ensure that you have understood the main takeaways that I intended for you.

A PERSONAL NOTE OF THANKS

Dear Readers,

As recruitment professionals, many of you may not know how many lives you have changed and how many people adore you. The purpose of this book is to make you sit back and realize that many of you have been role models for people you have met, interacted with, interviewed, and helped join their dream jobs.

If you have experienced a recruitment journey or aspire to become a recruiter, you should know that all recruitment professionals are the hidden gems in any organization, and I would like to thank each one of you for your passion for recruitment which is evident from the fact that you are holding this book.

INITIATION

1

HOW LIFE TEACHES US RECRUITMENT

I believe that everything you experience in life makes you a more learned person. Every moment, every hour, and every day you are learning something new, and learning becomes easier when you can relate it to real life.

I still remember the time when my father was looking for someone to join his startup in his early career. He was looking for someone who was a typing and photocopy expert, could open the shop, manage logistics and administrative activities, and could also manage finances in his absence. In a nutshell, he was looking for a full-stack professional, someone who could manage both front-end and back-end activities.

He issued advertisements inviting applications, conducted interviews through the applications, organized a walk-in event and asked his colleagues to share references. It took him around ten to fifteen days to find the right fit and that too through reference. When I look back at this thirty-year-old incident, I realize how, even without any formal knowledge of the recruitment process, he explored all possible aspects of it, be it walk-ins, job postings as an advertisement in a newspaper or referrals.

This made me understand how natural and intuitive the entire recruitment lifecycle is.

I THINK MATCHMAKING IS NOTHING LESS THAN A DOMESTIC FORM OF SOURCING TALENT AND FINALLY MAKING A PERMANENT ACQUISITION!

I believe that everything you experience in life makes you a more learned person. Every moment, every hour, and every day you are learning something new, and learning becomes easier when you can relate it with real life, and this is one of the biggest reasons why I love recruitment.

One of my aunts was an amazing sourcer; she learned how to use matrimonial sites to search for a groom for her daughter. She also learned all the ways of conducting advanced searches to get the desired lists of suitable matches for her daughter. I think matchmaking is nothing less than a domestic form of sourcing talent and finally making a permanent acquisition! People searching for perfect partners for their children or relatives become experts in conducting searches, marketing and describing the bio-data, which is as good as writing a job description.

2

A SOFTWARE ENGINEER TURNED RECRUITMENT PROFESSIONAL

Few things are meant to happen, and they create causes by themselves. I never thought that I would ever leave my cushy job till it happened.

A selfie lover, a social media enthusiast, a traveller, a writer, a mother, and a poet at heart—I am Parul Sharma, a recruitment professional working with Viasat as a global talent attraction and sourcing leader for the past three years. I embarked on the dream of authoring a book through an interesting roller coaster ride.

Born in the heart of India, Gwalior, Madhya Pradesh, I pursued my schooling in a small town in UP before finally returning to Gwalior for my engineering degree in 2002. Those miraculous four years of my life helped me realize my potential and my strengths and brought me closer to my dream of being independent and well-placed in my profession.

My college days were filled with excitement, fun, and learning as I pursued a degree in electronics and communication. The year 2006 did not favour us in terms of on-campus placements.

After graduating with honours, I was exploring job opportunities when destiny smiled upon me. I received news that Infosys was conducting an off-campus drive, and I received an invitation to appear for the entrance exam. It felt like destiny was in play; my preparations helped me crack the exams and interviews. I was selected as a Software Engineer and was placed in Chandigarh. With enthusiasm, I embarked on a journey of learning Java and various other related languages during the initial six months of my job.

As soon as I settled into my role, I was introduced to a new reporting tool, a completely unfamiliar territory compared to what I had learned. Undeterred, I embraced this challenge with determination, relying on user manuals and my innate curiosity. Remarkably, I not only mastered the tool but also began training my fellow team members. I worked on various projects and learned different languages and tools during my stint with Infosys.

Before I could even turn twenty-five, I was a well-settled married woman with a loving husband who, fortunately, turned out to be my best friend, thanks to our six months of courtship.

I believe that few things are meant to happen, creating their own causes. I never thought I would leave my cushy dream job until it happened. I had a choice in front of me after my marriage, either to leave my first job and move to Indore or continue to do the same job and stay in a different location, away from my husband. My family never agreed to the second option, and I decided to move on and leave my first job.

Looking back now, I realize that if that had not happened, this book would never have come into existence.

I was excited about stepping into a new life, but equally nervous about leaving my job. This time, my new location was Indore, and this move led me to an exciting opportunity—a chance to become a co-founder and technical lead at a startup: Rangrut Services India.

With excitement and a thirst for putting my knowledge into practice, I seized this opportunity. In my new role, I was responsible for everything from requirement gathering and documentation to development using PHP, MySQL, etc., and user testing. Moreover, I was entrusted with the task of building a team, and this task came surprisingly naturally to me.

I still remember the day in early 2009, when I received an email stating that we had a big project and that we needed to support a financial client with approximately two hundred hires. At that time, we were a team of around fifteen people, and we had a couple of projects to run. To my surprise, I was given the responsibility of hiring a team to support the hiring project. To help me accomplish this task, I was given access to a leading job portal in India, with hardly any training on how to use the job portal. Now all I had was the portal access, project details, and a deadline to start with the interview drive, line up the candidates for initial screening and provide the first set of shortlisted candidates in the next two weeks.

I was given two existing team members and was asked to hire an additional five recruiters in just two to three days. It sounded impossible to me, as I had to create a basic job description which was to be shared with candidates I was reaching out to. However, I did not get discouraged and started by referring to some of the existing job descriptions and drafting the new one according to the requirements. I made calls to candidates who appeared to be active job seekers and early joiners. I conducted short phone screening sessions to check their communication skills and relevant experience. I was even ready to hire a new graduate (fresher) if they could join early as they could be trained by experienced recruiters.

The impossible-looking task turned out to be a possibility as soon as I identified two recruiters for this project. They had previous experience of working on such projects and they started lining up candidates for the interview for our client on day one. Later we hired three other recruiters and this great team of five recruiters along with me supporting them, put our day and night into this project. In three months, we organized eight hundred interviews in different parts of the country and provided a list of around 225 shortlisted candidates. The project, which initially looked like moving a mountain, I realized was actually a set of stones which needed to be moved, one stone at a time. All we needed was hard work and a great team.

As time passed, I found myself delving deeper into the world of recruitment, a journey that seemed to unfold effortlessly. Soon, I was using job portals to build a database, tackling various recruitment requirements, and even handling recruitment-related projects. It was a natural progression, a path I had not planned on but wholeheartedly embraced.

As I recount this journey, I do not want to miss sharing with you an incident which both shocked and moved me. I was given the task of hiring a senior director for one of our banking clients. This was a difficult role to fill, and I had no experience in hiring for leadership roles. I started with the thought that I could do it, no matter what. I reached out to several

> **THE BIGGEST LESSON I LEARNED WAS THAT NOTHING IS CERTAIN, AND IN THE END, WE CANNOT CONTROL EVERYTHING, NO MATTER HOW HARD WE TRY.**

potential candidates but couldn't find anyone relevant to the position. I spoke to almost twenty-five people and reviewed almost seventy to eighty resumes. After conducting a few interviews, we finally selected one, and I was delighted. It was not an ordinary selection for me. This entire process took almost two months. I had heard that until someone reached the venue for joining formalities, anything could happen, and take you back to square one. In most cases, we had a backup candidate in mind, but we had not found one in this case.

On the day of joining, I made a follow-up call to the selected candidate. He did not respond, and I thought I had lost this position, and my efforts were in vain. I made another attempt to contact him, keeping my fingers crossed. This time the phone was picked up, but a lady answered the call. I asked if I could speak to Akhil. She whispered, and I could not hear her. I asked her again if I could speak to him as he was supposed to join a new role today and what I heard made me go numb. I was told that Akhil had met with an accident while driving to the new workplace and he was no longer with us. I was deeply saddened by this news. The biggest lesson I learned was that nothing is certain, and in the end, we cannot control everything, no matter how hard we try. We conveyed the information to our client and continued with our day. We were working the whole day, but there was silence. I can still feel that silence within.

Within the next few days, we got back to normal, but this incident left a void in us. I learned that day that it is good to trust the commitments made by candidates in terms of joining the organization on the expected date and time, but we cannot rely blindly on them as there are multiple external factors involved.

One day, driven by a desire to learn from industry leaders, my founding team and I reached out to Mr N.R. Narayana Murthy, a founding member of Infosys Technologies.

Getting an appointment with Mr Murthy was not an easy task; we found a way to reach his PA, Mr Pandu. He was a kind person and after some e-mail exchanges and explaining the purpose of the meeting, I got an appointment to meet him for an hour in Bengaluru. By this time, I was no longer an employee of Infosys, but I still felt a sense of belonging. Also, the thought of a face-to-face interview with Mr Murthy gave me goosebumps.

I entered Infosys Bengaluru for the first time on the day of my meeting. It was an amazing experience for me and my husband who accompanied me on this important day.

I went inside a conference room and within a minute, the stalwart of this industry walked in with diligence. I asked him what he thought of my startup and how he thought we could add value to early placements. All I can say is that I got very insightful views which helped me a lot in my recruitment career. It was one of the most special days of my life and those moments continue to stay with me forever.

One of the most valuable insights that he shared was his views on the scalability of businesses.

He mentioned, "One of the biggest factors contributing to the success

ONE OF THE BIGGEST FACTORS CONTRIBUTING TO THE SUCCESS OF A CORPORATION IS HANDLING SCALABILITY.

of a corporation is handling scalability. How do you make sure that you are able to produce more widgets or more software, how are you able to satisfy more customers and how do you ensure as against four hundred projects last year, you are able to handle four thousand projects this year while retaining quality and productivity? Similarly, how do you process one hundred thousand applications and select perhaps ten thousand people?" He shared that to do this, we have to use technology and systems. We must use human innovation and train our talent. This way, we would be able to scale up our recruitment process.

Everything he mentioned that day makes perfect sense, even today. I can see how successful organizations rely heavily on a recruitment function which is scalable.

Over the next seven years, I did everything in my power to contribute to my organization's success and my personal growth. In 2010, I decided to broaden my horizons and enrolled in an

Executive Management Program at IIM Bangalore, designed specifically for entrepreneurs. This program expanded my understanding of workforce management, business planning, supply, and demand dynamics, and marketing strategies. It was during this journey that I realized the transformative potential of recruitment in any business.

By the end of 2015, I had evolved into a seasoned recruitment professional, adept at hiring for a wide range of skills and industries. I was ready for a new challenge.

3

CHANGING WITH CHALLENGING TIMES

Your career is like a garden. It can hold an assortment of life's energy that yields a bounty for you. You do not need to grow just one thing in your garden. You do not need to do just one thing in your career.

—Jennifer Ritchie Payette

Having spent more than seven years at my startup, I started feeling that this was the right time to get back into the corporate world. I wanted to put everything I had learned into practice. I started preparing for job interviews and got an opportunity to join a mid-level IT company as a retainer for six months. This job opened another set of opportunities for me. While I was serving my final days of retainership, I was exploring opportunities for my next move and this led me to Capgemini, India, where I took on the role of a sourcing consultant.

My professional journey has taught me that if you wish for something, you need to continue to plan in that direction and prepare yourself to achieve what you are striving for.

After Infosys, Capgemini India was another company I had aspired to work for. Even before I joined, I was sure that I was about to embark on an exciting journey.

I was interviewed by a few of the best professionals who valued my stint with a startup. I found myself surrounded by an incredible team of sourcing and recruitment experts, enriching my knowledge and skills in various facets of talent acquisition.

The best part about the team at Capgemini was their passion for sourcing and talent attraction. The team was always excited about new tools and platforms, and the head of the function was a great motivator for the team. I got to work with some amazing leaders who always encouraged and motivated me to explore new methods of sourcing and recruitment. I was soon appointed as a sourcer for the Centre of Excellence (CoE) for one of the most critical businesses 'Insights and Data' where we got to hire talent for the most critical and niche roles and skills.

We used to get requests for positions and skills we had never heard of. There were times when we had to google the skills and then get on business calls! However, to our surprise, they would tell us that even they were hiring for those skills for the first time and had no idea about the pool availability.

It was challenging, but I must admit it was fun and it pushed us to not limit ourselves to regular job portals and postings.

Parallelly, there were skills that were highly sought after, like the working experience of Hadoop and Informatica. To target high numbers of applicants for these roles, we also used to conduct weekend interviews called walk-in drives.

In 2020, life took us all for a rollercoaster ride, both on the personal and professional front. People lost their jobs or loved ones or both due to COVID-19. The lockdown and the subsequent work from home had a positive impact too as new businesses started to flourish and people went back to their hometowns to be with their families.

Most organizations moved to virtual meetings on platforms such as MS Teams, Zoom, Google Meet, etc., and these became the new normal ways of meeting people. Schools, colleges, yoga, aerobics, and other things completely went online. My biggest worry in those times was the increasing demand for talent in various fields. Specifically, the talent we had to find within a specified turnaround time. Since we were not going to have any face-to-face weekend drives for at least a few months, we moved to conducting more interviews on weekdays, which always had its own limitations in terms of meeting the expected footfall.

During COVID-19, the biggest requirement of companies who had huge hiring plans was to have something which could replace the weekend walk-in drives or campus drives virtually.

If I go back to 2019 and visualize a full-fledged weekend drive, all I remember is the footfall of candidates, panel members for technical interviews, feedback forms, candidates' resumes, interview rooms, whole-day coordination, etc. It was difficult to imagine something to replicate this model virtually until I came across an amazing platform called an elevator (also known as a superset). This turned out to be a replica of weekend walk-in drives with the following facilities:

Virtual interview rooms where panel members can connect with candidates on a video call, **online feedback forms** with predefined competencies to rate the candidates, and **candidate resumes** which are visible to the interviewing panel as soon as

WE USED TO GET REQUESTS FOR POSITIONS AND SKILLS WE HAD NEVER HEARD OF. THERE WERE TIMES WHEN WE HAD TO GOOGLE THE SKILLS AND THEN GET ON BUSINESS CALLS!

the candidate is moved to the interview room by the drive coordinator. There was also an **online interview venue** which gets created after posting the requirement where the link is generated which is shared with candidates through mails. **The availability of candidates** is visible to the coordinators through colourful icons along with the preferred time slots.

The tool was extremely user-friendly, both before and after the interviews. All the interview recordings were saved and could be accessed later whenever needed. Also, it gave us the facility to download candidate profiles, along with all the required details and feedback. The best part of being online was that there were no location constraints.

I experienced these virtual weekends where we were able to get a good number of candidates with reduced paperwork and increased automation. Candidates sitting in Coimbatore could attend interviews organized for Chennai or Bengaluru without any travel. We would get a snapshot of the progress of interviews, selections, footfall, and the entire summary by the end of the day.

This made me wonder if we really needed to arrange such drives face-to-face when we could do it much more efficiently online. I was sure that this gave everyone a lot of flexibility, options, comfort, and opportunities. Every challenge that we face is an opportunity to become more than we have been before. We landed in a virtual world with more perfection and productivity.

Getting back to my story, destiny had many more experiences in store for me. I spent over five years in this wonderful organization. Through one of my close friends, I learned about an exciting opportunity at a satellite giant Viasat, and the role seemed tailored for me.

As I said, great people make great companies. This was going to be another such workplace.

Viasat turned out to be a hidden gem, valuing not only my professional skills but also my personal worth. It provided me with opportunities at every step, motivation, and the balance I needed to accomplish my goals.

During my years at Viasat, I realized how a great team operates and that it does not matter where the team is located. If you have a vision to deliver and a purpose to perform, time and location are just specifics.

And so, my story continues, as I shaped my career, contributed to my organization, and got inspired by those around me. My journey is a testament to the idea that everything happens for a reason, and each experience prepares us for the next chapter in our lives.

EVERY CHALLENGE THAT WE FACE IS THE OPPORTUNITY TO BECOME MORE THAN WE HAVE BEEN BEFORE.

4

RECRUITMENT IN A NUTSHELL

Reviewing the applications of sourced or attracted candidates is like preparing and organizing your ingredients before cooking.

Before we deep dive into the basics of recruitment, I would like to define recruitment for you. It is simple, but important. Since this contains the essence of the book, let me relate it to an everyday activity for easier understanding.

In one of my interactions with my husband, who is a great cook and works in the recruitment field, I realized that the recruitment process is very similar to cooking! Just as cooking delicious food requires certain steps, recruiting too requires certain steps to be followed:

1. **Job Description (Recipe):** A well-defined job description is similar to a detailed recipe with all listed ingredients. An incomplete recipe may lead to a not-so-tasty dish and an improper job description may lead to irrelevant applications.

2. **Sourcing and Attracting Candidates (Collecting Ingredients):** Just as we must collect or shop for ingredients before we get down to cooking, we need to

source and attract the right kind of candidates for the recruiting process.

3. **Screening Candidates (Preparation):** Reviewing the applications of sourced or attracted candidates is like preparing and organizing your ingredients before you cook. If you start cooking before collecting all the ingredients, you might end up spoiling the dish. The taste will be compromised and there will be an additional fuel cost involved.

4. **Interviews (Cooking):** Just like in cooking, as soon as we have the recipe (job description), ingredients (candidates) and preparations done (screening), we start the interview process where we assess the quality of candidates for hiring.

5. **Selection (Tasting the Dish):** Selecting the right candidate is as good as tasting the dish before the final presentation to check if we can meet the expectations of the hiring manager.

6. **Onboarding (Presentation):** Onboarding the new hire is similar to presenting the dish to our client. A good candidate's experience is as good as a good presentation of the dish.

My purpose in authoring this book is to take you through the recipe and ingredients of the recruitment process and give you a sneak peek at the other side of the table. As a recruiter, we have full control of the job descriptions, candidate sourcing and attraction, and screening of candidates before we present the candidates to the hiring manager. Interviews and selection process completely depend on the three steps of recruiting (job descriptions, sourcing and attracting candidates, and screening the applications).

The next chapter will help you create a perfect recipe to start this wonderful journey of recruitment.

5

CANDIDATE RECRUITMENT LIFECYCLE

Our experience of a good movie or good food is not just limited to the outcome, but it starts the moment we step into a theatre or a restaurant. The ambience, the staff, promptness to queries, and the service along with the outcome – all of it adds to the experience.

Attraction, connection, engagement, and experience are the four defining pillars of the recruitment life cycle for any candidate and for any organization.

Not only does an organization need to attract candidates, connect with them, engage with them, and give them a great experience to make sure that they become part of the organization, but it is also important to be able to attract candidates who align with the culture, values, mission, and goals of the organization.

It is important to understand the vision, career goals, value system, work ethics, team collaboration, adaptability, flexibility, and leadership potential of every candidate who is going through the recruitment life cycle.

It is worth describing these important parameters of the recruitment life cycle.

ATTRACTING CANDIDATES

The first step of the recruitment life cycle is attracting candidates. At this stage, we need to market our employer's brand and job and have a strong employee value proposition. The primary goal is not only to attract the right talent but also to encourage them to apply for open positions. We will be covering in our next chapters how we can attract candidates by leveraging various channels, such as job portals, social media platforms, and employee referrals.

CONNECTING WITH CANDIDATES

The second step of the recruitment life cycle is connecting with candidates where we need to review resumes and reach out to potential candidates for screening and initial interviews. It is crucial to keep the communication lines open and provide a positive candidate experience. To further engage with the candidate during the recruitment process and provide a great experience, it is important to connect with the candidate through conversation and by offering suitable job opportunities to them.

We always initiate our conversations with 'happy to connect' but do we really intend to 'stay connected' for a long-term purpose? When we initiate connections through networking or through phone calls, it is important to keep in mind that you are not working to close one single position with one hire, but you are preparing your connections for future roles as well.

ENGAGING WITH CANDIDATES

The third step of the recruitment life cycle is engaging with candidates where we need to focus on building a relationship with them, sharing information about the organization and evaluating the candidate's fit for the job and company culture. This stage includes conducting further interviews, assessment tests, and reference checks. In case the candidate is a great fit in terms of culture and is interested in your organization, but you do not have any job to be offered as per their skills, you may consider the candidate for future roles.

PROVIDING A GOOD CANDIDATE EXPERIENCE

The final step of the recruitment life cycle is providing a good candidate experience which starts from the day you plan your attraction strategy and set up the stage for candidates to experience the process of applying for the job, receiving the first communication mail from recruiters, first conversation with the recruiter, the interview process to offer discussions, onboarding and salary negotiations.

It is the same as the fact that our experience of a good movie or good food is not just limited to the outcome of the story of the movie or the taste of the food, but it starts the moment we step into the theatre or a restaurant. The ambience, the staff, guidance at each step and the service along with the outcome – all of it adds to the experience.

So, in the recruitment life cycle, every step should be executed keeping the candidate's experience in mind. Here are a few tips for each step:

❖ **Attraction and Application:** The first touch point with the candidate is the job description. If that is written well, you will be successful in attracting the candidate to the career page to complete the job application.

Providing a flawless application experience is important when a candidate finds it easy to apply for the role. The upcoming chapter about job descriptions will provide more insights into a well-written job description.

❖ **Screening and Interview Process:** Once the candidate has completed the application process, the next opportunity to provide a good experience comes during the phone screening process. How you initiate the conversation becomes the point where the candidate sets up the expectations of the upcoming processes.

❖ **Continuous Engagement:** When the candidate is undergoing technical and HR interviews, it is important for the recruiter to be the single point of contact who can provide regular updates and feedback during the interview process.

❖ **Making a Job Offer:** Once the candidate has been identified for the position, we move to the next step of making a job offer to the candidate. At that time, it is important to explain to them the details of the job like the start date, hours, location and pay. The offer should be clear and should mention all the important details, including the compensation details and the benefits offered.

❖ **Negotiating Salary:** Sometimes, or rather most of the time, candidates may negotiate the salary or benefits before accepting the offer. Recruiters or human resource professionals who are discussing the final offer should be open to negotiating, considering the budget for the role and the candidate's worth to the organization. No matter what, the negotiation should be conducted respectfully and professionally.

❖ **Onboarding Process:** Once the candidate accepts the job offer, we get into the onboarding phase. This candidate will soon be a part of the organization and will be introduced to the organization's culture, values, and policies. The onboarding process should be well-structured and informative so that the employee starts the job with all the information they need.

❖ **Feedback to Candidate:** Giving timely feedback and maintaining a relationship with candidates can help create a positive image of the organization. Even if the candidates are not selected for a particular role, a good experience will encourage them to share good feedback about the organization which in turn strengthens the brand and sets up the platform to attract more talent.

In a nutshell, the candidate recruitment life cycle is a continuous process that requires a strategic approach to attract, connect, engage, and provide a good candidate experience. By focusing on each stage of the recruitment process, we can build a positive employer brand, attract top talent, and find the best candidate for the job who also values the organization and its culture.

In the upcoming chapters, you will learn in detail about a few of the most important functions of this recruitment life cycle.

LET'S SYNTHESIZE

Do you remember any incident as a recruiter which made you feel proud of your profession? As an aspiring recruiter, do you remember any awe-inspiring incident regarding this profession?

....

....

....

....

....

Do you remember incidents in your day-to-day life which relate very closely to the recruitment process?

....

....

....

....

....

What is your definition of recruitment?

....

....

....

....

....

TALENT ATTRACTION AND RECRUITMENT MARKETING

6

DESCRIBING WHAT WE WANT: THE JOB DESCRIPTION

A robust job description is like a magnet for top talent – attracting candidates by illuminating the role's essence, expectations, and the value they can bring to the table.

Have you ever scrolled through a matrimonial website and found yourself reading the characteristics of an ideal match? It is striking how similar it is to a job description! Whether it be business analysis, software development, or construction of buildings, before diving into any project, it is important to first define what you want. This process, known as requirement gathering and documentation, ensures that you are clear on your client's expectations and can deliver accordingly.

Similarly, crafting the perfect job description is crucial for any organization or employer looking to hire the right candidate. A job description, like a perfect recipe, outlines the roles and responsibilities of the job, the required qualifications and experience, and any other relevant details. It serves as the first communication between an employer and a potential employee, so it is important that it is precise and clear.

Before giving more details about how to write effective job descriptions and job titles which are search engine optimized, we need to know a few things regarding the attention span of job seekers:

According to Microsoft, the digital world has reduced our attention span to eight seconds. Just eight seconds!

The following key points will help you draft the most effective job description:

1. Search Engine Optimization (SEO) Friendly Job Titles
2. Google Trends for Evaluating Job Titles
3. Features of a Good Job Description: Do's & Don'ts
4. Sample Standard Job Description
5. Impact

1. SEO-FRIENDLY JOB TITLES

❖ Making job titles search engine optimized means that as soon as the candidate searches for any job on search engines like Google, Bing etc., the jobs with more accurate job descriptions and job titles will appear on the first page. Consider the **profile of the ideal candidate** and what you imagine they will type in on the search engine while looking for a job.

❖ Apart from the job title, the **location of the job is another important keyword** to include because most people search by job title and location.

❖ The title of your posting must be to the point. It is going to give a clear indication, to both search engines and job seekers, of **what the job role is all about**.

❖ The job title is not just a title, it is **a marketing**

headline. Do not list job titles that are different, like 'Chief Creativity Officer', 'Sourcing Ninja', 'Gung-ho Programmer', etc. These phrases are considered negative keywords and can impact the results.

❖ Never use generic job titles like software developer, programmer, or tester. They may not attract the right set of applicants.

2. GOOGLE TRENDS FOR EVALUATING JOB TITLES

Google Trends is a powerful and free tool that provides insights into the popularity and search interest of specific keywords or topics over time. It can be a valuable resource for job seekers, employers, and recruiters to understand the demand for different job titles and industries. Here is how you can utilize Google Trends for appropriate job titles:

❖ **Explore Job Title Trends**
   Go to the Google Trends website (trends.google.com).
   In the search bar, enter one or more job titles or job-related keywords that you want to research. For example, 'Data Scientist', 'Marketing Manager', or 'Software Engineer'.

❖ **Refine Your Search**
   Use filters: Google Trends allows you to filter results by location, time, category (e.g., jobs and education), and type of search (e.g., web search, image search, news search). You can tailor your search to specific regions or time frames.

❖ **Compare Job titles**
   You can compare the search interest for multiple job titles by separating them with commas in the search

bar. For example, you can compare 'Data Scientist' and 'Data Analyst' to see which one is more popular.

❖ **Analyze the Data**

Google Trends will provide you with a visual representation of search interest over time. You will see a graph with data points.

Pay attention to spikes or trends in the graph. These can indicate times when a particular job title is in high demand or experiencing increased interest.

Look for seasonal patterns or long-term trends. Some job titles may have fluctuations based on the time of year or industry changes.

❖ **Geographical Insights**

You can also see where the highest search interest for a specific job title is located geographically. This can be helpful if you are considering relocating for a job or targeting a specific location for your job search.

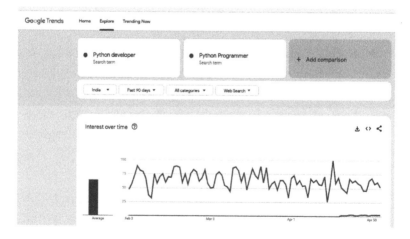

3. FEATURES OF A GOOD JOB DESCRIPTIONS

A good job description not only helps in attracting the right candidates but also assists in finding the best match for the position, as the candidate has a clear understanding of what is expected of them.

Highlight the Job Title and Location

The job title and location are usually the first pieces of information candidates look for in a job description. This information should be placed prominently at the beginning to clarify which position you are hiring for and where the position is located.

Talk about the Mission, Vision, Values, Culture, and Growth Plan of the Organization

Sharing your organization's mission, vision, values, culture, and future plan for growth is important to provide context and insight into what the company stands for and where it is headed.

- ❖ **Mission:** The mission statement defines the company's primary purpose and its reason for existence. It explains what the company does and for whom.

- ❖ **Vision:** The vision statement outlines the company's long-term goals and aspirations. It describes the desired future state the company aims to achieve.

- ❖ **Values:** Company values reflect the core principles and beliefs that guide decision-making and behaviour within the organization. Values can include integrity, innovation, teamwork, etc.

❖ **Culture:** Describing the company culture gives candidates a sense of the work environment, including its atmosphere, work ethic, and employee relationships.

❖ **Growth Plan:** Explaining the organization's plan for growth provides insight into potential career development opportunities and where the company is headed in the future.

Roles and Responsibilities

This section should provide detailed information about what the job entails. It is important to outline:

❖ **Project:** Describe the projects the candidate will be involved in; their scope and objectives.

❖ **Team:** Explain the team structure, who the candidate will be working with, and their role within the team.

❖ **Job Responsibilities:** List specific tasks and responsibilities the candidate will be expected to perform. Use bullet points for clarity.

Required Skills and Preferences

This section outlines the skills and qualifications needed for the role.

❖ **Required Skills:** Mention the essential skills and qualifications that candidates must possess to be considered for the position. These are non-negotiable.

❖ **Preferences:** These are additional skills or qualifications that would be beneficial but are not mandatory. Preferences can include certifications, industry-specific experience, or specialized skills.

Additional Details

This section provides any extra information that is relevant to the job or the application process.

- ❖ **Location Flexibility:** Specify if there is flexibility regarding the job location, such as the possibility of remote work or different office locations.
- ❖ **Educational Qualification:** State the minimum educational requirements for the position, including any preferred degrees or certifications.
- ❖ **Citizenship Status:** If applicable, mention whether the company requires candidates to have a specific citizenship status or work authorization.

Inclusive Job Description to Attract a Larger Audience

- ❖ Inclusivity is important in job descriptions to encourage a diverse pool of applicants.
- ❖ Use inclusive language that welcomes candidates from different backgrounds, genders, ages, and abilities.
- ❖ Highlight the company's commitment to diversity and inclusion.
- ❖ Avoid using biased language or criteria that may discourage certain groups from applying.

Breakdown Description into Bullet Points

- ❖ Using bullet points makes the job description more scannable and reader-friendly.
- ❖ It helps candidates identify key information and responsibilities quickly.
- ❖ Each bullet point should be concise and focus on a specific aspect of the job or qualifications.

❖ Creating a well-structured job description with these elements can attract qualified candidates and set clear expectations for the role.

✦ Inconsistent sequencing: Once the flow is set, all job descriptions must be in the same format.

✦ Avoid using jargon which is specific to internal groups.

✦ There should be no spelling mistakes or grammatical errors.

✦ The job description should not be gender-biased.

✦ Avoid never-ending paragraphs.

4. SAMPLE JOB DESCRIPTION

In my college days, I learned how important it was to go to labs to conduct practical sessions and try to execute everything we learned in our theory classes. Theory was important for reference, but executing what was taught always helped to strengthen the concepts. This principle always motivates me to present concepts with examples.

It would not be fair to conclude this chapter without an example of how a job description can be drafted with the above-discussed specifications. Remember, there are no thumb rules for a perfect job description, but we can still set the tone with a sample job description given below.

Job Title: Talent Attraction Manager

Location: [City, State]

About Us:

At XYZ Company, we are on a mission to revolutionize the industry through an innovative talent attraction strategy. Our vision is to become a global leader in our field by consistently delivering top-notch solutions to our clients. We are guided by a set of core values, including creativity, integrity, and teamwork, which form the foundation of our company culture. As we continue to grow, we are looking for a Talent Attraction Manager to join our team and play a pivotal role in our exciting journey towards excellence.

ROLES AND RESPONSIBILITIES

- ❖ Lead the development and execution of comprehensive talent attraction strategies that align with the company's goals and objectives.
- ❖ Manage and mentor a team of talent attraction and sourcing professionals, providing guidance and support to ensure the successful implementation of attraction campaigns.
- ❖ Conduct market research and analysis to identify trends and opportunities and use data-driven insights to inform decisions.
- ❖ Collaborate cross-functionally with hiring managers, recruiters, and other teams to ensure a cohesive and integrated attraction approach.
- ❖ Create and manage attraction budgets, track ROI, and report on key performance metrics to senior management.
- ❖ Oversee the development of creative content, including

social media campaigns, social media content, and email marketing initiatives.

❖ Stay up to date with industry trends and best practices to continuously improve the effectiveness of talent attraction efforts.

REQUIRED SKILLS

❖ Bachelor's degree in marketing, business, or a related field. An MBA is a plus.

❖ Proven experience as a talent acquisition or attraction manager or similar role, with a track record of successful attraction campaigns.

❖ Strong leadership and team management skills.

❖ Excellent communication and interpersonal abilities.

❖ Proficiency in recruitment marketing tools and platforms.

❖ Analytical mindset with the ability to interpret data and make data-driven decisions.

PREFERENCES

❖ Certification in recruitment or related fields.

❖ Familiarity with the use of AI in recruiting.

❖ Creative thinking and problem-solving skills.

ADDITIONAL DETAILS

❖ Location flexibility: This position is based in [City, State], but remote work options may be considered for the right candidate.

❖ Educational Qualification: A bachelor's degree in marketing, business, or a related field is required. An MBA is preferred.

❖ Citizenship Status: Open to candidates with legal authorization to work in [Country].

WHY JOIN US

We are committed to building a diverse and inclusive workplace. We welcome applications from individuals of all backgrounds and experiences. We believe that diversity fosters innovation and creativity, and we encourage candidates of all races, genders, ages, and abilities to apply.

Disclaimer: This is not a company-specific job description and is created for illustrative purposes only.

5. IMPACT

Just like a good trailer can entice you to watch a movie, a good job description can attract the right candidates and help in finding the best match for the position. A good job description helps in:

❖ Better search engine optimization of the job;
❖ Increase in relevant applications of candidates;
❖ Increased attention span of job seekers;
❖ A strong step towards a strategic recruitment marketing approach.

So, if you are a recruiter or are willing to understand this process, take some time to draft a job description that accurately reflects the position and reflects your organization's culture and benefits.

If you are a job seeker, remember to read beyond the job title and carefully review the job description before applying.

LET'S SYNTHESIZE

Have you come across any job descriptions which impressed you and left a lasting impact on you? If yes, what were the things which caught your attention?

....

....

....

....

Would you be able to define your roles and responsibilities as a recruiter in eight to ten bullet points?

....

....

....

....

Try analyzing five different job titles of your preference versus what other organizations use in general. Review what's trending.

....

....

....

....

....

....

What as per you will have more ratings on Google? Talent Acquisition or Recruitment? Try it out!

....

....

....

....

....

7

TOOLS AND PLATFORMS FOR SOURCING AND ATTRACTING TALENT

We exhibit remarkable detective skills in uncovering information about our dear ones, and in the realm of recruitment, we not only excel in this, but are also recognized and rewarded for this skill.

I believe that we should explore all platforms to attract and reach out to the right talent. Any platform left unexplored indicates a missed opportunity to reach a candidate who could have been a perfect hire for the role.

All of us turn out to be very good detectives when it comes to finding more information for or about our loved ones and in recruitment, we are praised and paid for this. You need to find people who will love the job you are offering.

Let's rewind a little. When it comes to finding a perfect match for our family members, we do everything from reference to leg work to using matrimonial websites to whatnot!

We are natural sourcers when it comes to finding something for ourselves. We are eager to explore different methods which help us in fulfilling our desires quickly. However, we might need to put in additional effort when our choices are unique or niche.

We are fortunate enough to have multiple platforms and artificial intelligence based tools to find the people we are looking for. We have the right match just a click away from us, but do we know where to find them?

Talent Attraction and Sourcing play the most important role in finding the purple squirrel for our positions. Attracting something is pull-based and the same concept applies to attracting talent where we follow all steps to attract the best talent through pull strategies, whereas sourcing talent is a strategy where we apply some push as well and try to reach out to the right talent.

Before we talk about sourcing in detail, I would like to define it here. Sourcing, rather 'talent sourcing', is the process of searching or finding potential candidates through various channels, such as job boards, social media, professional networking sites, and employee referrals.

Ninety per cent of the time, sourcing is not about how to source but where to source from.

If you know where to source from, you will indeed learn how to source, and these skills are trainable.

In addition, there are various tools we can use for different purposes, including sourcing, job posting, talent insights, social media recruitment and so on.

SOURCING AND JOB POSTING TOOLS

We have multiple platforms to source candidates we wish to hire, map the talent and pull out market insights.

There are various job boards available which facilitate the search for candidates with specific educational qualifications, location, skills, and experience. Job boards not only give us access to the professional profile and details of all the candidates in the form of a resume, but they also help us find candidates who are actively looking for a job change.

We can attract candidates through job boards or can also plan to market our jobs through job postings.

Most job boards have features to connect with candidates through mail/messaging or provide us with contact details of the candidates so that we can connect with them through mail/SMS/calls/chats.

I have used many of the below-listed job boards and have heard about others from different networking events and platforms. I have tried to give you a quick understanding of these platforms but would recommend deep diving into details by visiting their websites.

- ❖ **Indeed:** It is a popular job search engine among recruiters. Indeed aggregates job listings from various sources, making it a go-to platform for job seekers. It also provides various filters to refine the search results.

- ❖ **Glassdoor:** This platform not only allows you to post job openings directly through a career website but also provides insights into company reviews and ratings, which can attract more informed candidates interested in your company's culture.

- ❖ **Monster:** It is a traditional job portal that offers a wide range of job posting options and features for reaching a diverse candidate pool. It also provides filters to refine search results and review applicants against job postings.

- ❖ **CareerBuilder:** Similar to other job portals, Career Builder also offers various tools and options for posting job openings, sourcing, and reaching candidates.
- ❖ **SimplyHired:** Like Indeed, SimplyHired is a job search engine that collects job listings from all over the web, including company career pages, job boards, and niche job websites.
- ❖ **Naukri:** A well-known recruitment job portal in India, Naukri provides recruitment solutions to corporates and placement agencies and a wide variety of job openings to job seekers in India.
- ❖ **Dice:** Dice specializes in technical and Information Technology job postings.
- ❖ **Hired:** This platform provides access to technical and non-technical candidates through job postings and branding options.
- ❖ **Clearancejobs:** If you are hiring in the US for positions which require different types of clearance requirements like Secret Clearance or Top Secret clearance as a part of any security clearance, this is the right platform for you.

There are many more efficient tools which help recruiters find and attract suitable candidates.

The effectiveness of each platform certainly varies depending on the industry, location, and the type of position you are looking to fill.

It is always a good idea to do your research and choose the platforms that align best with your target audience. Additionally, you need to consider the cost, features, and user experience offered by each platform when making your decision.

Professional Networking and Social Media Tools: One of the biggest professional networking platforms with more than 820 million registered users is LinkedIn. Most of us, irrespective of recruiting background, understand LinkedIn and its importance.

❖ **LinkedIn and LinkedIn Recruiter:** LinkedIn provides an opportunity to connect with like-minded professionals, colleagues, and friends.

It also provides an option for following leaders across the globe. With such a huge presence of professionals, LinkedIn has become the largest platform which connects employers and candidates through jobs. It provides a job search and job posting platform named LinkedIn Recruiter.

LinkedIn Recruiter is an extensive hiring platform for talent professionals that helps find, connect with, and manage the people you want on your team. You will get up-to-date insights on more than 770 million members, advanced search filters, and recommended matches to prioritize based on who is most open to hearing from you.

Most of the tools mentioned above provide multiple features like search capabilities, candidate engagement, candidate management, integration with an Applicant Tracking System (ATS) etc. We will talk separately about ATS in the coming chapters. Let's consider these features with respect to LinkedIn Recruiter.

Search capabilities: This platform helps find qualified candidates through its advanced search filters, both locally and internationally.

Candidate Engagement: It provides features to engage with candidates through personalized InMails and helps save time by providing bulk action and customizable templates. The AI-driven InMail templates make it very convenient for recruiters to connect with candidates.

Candidate Management: Apart from all the sourcing, searching and job posting features, LinkedIn Recruiter provides a candidate management platform through LinkedIn Projects.

LinkedIn Projects: This feature helps recruiters manage all the sourcing activities in one place. It can accommodate all saved searches, job postings, job applicants, candidate pipelines and leads generated from any campaign in one place. These projects help you share the candidate details or the entire project directly with the hiring manager and provide them with the option of reviewing candidates.

Integration with ATS: LinkedIn Recruiter can be integrated with ATS which helps recruiters perform most of the screening and sourcing activities directly from LinkedIn. Through this feature, a shortlisted profile can directly be uploaded on the ATS, and the candidate's status can be loaded against the candidate's profile on LinkedIn which helps save a lot of time.

❖ **HireEz Recruiter:** HireEz, previously known as Hiretual, is an AI-powered recruitment platform which helps source from more than forty-five platforms. Similar to LinkedIn, it also provides search capabilities, candidate management, candidate engagement, and ATS integration capabilities. The candidate engagement in HireEz is also AI-driven which makes it easier for recruiters to connect and engage with candidates at different stages. HireEz also provides facilities like a Boolean builder or job description parsing for ease of sourcing and searching candidates. There is a lot we can explore while using these tools.

Over and above the traditional job boards and networking tools, social media platforms can be utilized to make job postings. This broadens our reach and helps tap into different candidate demographics. All we need is to tailor our posts to suit each platform's audience. Here are some examples of social media channels that can be used to make job postings:

❖ **Facebook:** Based on candidate demographics, Facebook can help us reach a wider range of candidates. We can create targeted ads based on location, interests, demographics and more.

❖ **X (Previously known as Twitter):** For quick job postings and reaching tech-savvy or media-focused candidates, X is a quick go-to platform. One needs to use relevant hashtags to expand the reach of posts.

❖ **Instagram:** For attracting early graduates, the younger generation, and candidates who are more inclined towards creative and art fields, Instagram is a highly effective platform. Being more visual and engaging, Instagram can help in showcasing our company culture and highlighting the benefits of working with our organization.

❖ **YouTube:** You can create quick video content through regular videos or YouTube shorts to showcase your company culture, employee stories, and job role descriptions. You can even post video job descriptions with a quick introduction to the roles through these videos.

❖ **Snapchat:** This platform is well suited for temporary roles or intern positions, considering the audience demographics and its focus on quick and engaging content.

❖ **WhatsApp:** Especially useful for local or regional job postings, WhatsApp allows for direct communication with potential candidates. I have personally found it effective for the quick turnaround time of candidate responses.

It is always advised to modify your content for each platform's audience and format it based on a candidate's demographics. You can use visuals, videos, and messaging apps to capture the attention of job seekers. You also need to monitor your engagement and plan your future postings based on the performance of your posts on each platform.

PLATFORMS TO MAP TALENT

There are platforms which help you find candidates and then there are platforms which help you map the talent. Whenever you read a book, you always refer to the table of contents. Similarly, platforms like HireEZ, Seekout, Talent Neuron, and LinkedIn Insights provide you with a snapshot of the talent availability based on location, skills, experience range, qualification and so on. They give you detailed insights on desired skills versus the available talent pool. These platforms enable recruiters and hiring managers to make decisions based on the pool available.

- ❖ **LinkedIn Talent Insights:** This tool leverages data from LinkedIn's vast professional network to provide detailed insights into workforce trends, talent availability and emerging skills. It allows us to explore talent pools, understand competitor talent strategies and identify potential candidates based on various criteria.

- ❖ **Glassdoor:** Glassdoor offers not only company reviews and ratings but also provides insights into job market trends, salary data, and competitor analysis. It helps organizations understand how they compare to competitors in terms of attracting and retaining talent.

- ❖ **TalentNeuron by Gartner:** This tool provides global talent market insights, helping organizations make data-driven decisions related to workforce planning, talent acquisition, and skill development. It offers insights into talent supply and demand, salary benchmarks, and workforce trends. It also rates hiring difficulty on a scale of one to ten, with ten being the most difficult.

- ❖ **Entelo:** Entelo combines AI and machine learning to help organizations identify and engage with potential candidates. It searches various online sources to find relevant candidate information and provides insights into the talent landscape, diversity hiring, and market trends.

❖ **Hired:** Hired is a platform that connects technological talent with companies. It offers insights into the availability of tech talent, compensation trends, and skill demand in the technology industry.

❖ **TalentLyft:** This tool offers a comprehensive recruitment platform that includes features for talent mapping and insights. It helps organizations source candidates, build talent pipelines and analyze recruitment data to optimize their hiring processes.

❖ **Dice Insights:** Focused on the technology industry, Dice Insights provides data and insights into tech talent trends, skill demand, and market dynamics. It assists organizations in understanding the evolving tech talent landscape.

❖ **Talentsoft:** Talentsoft offers a talent management suite that includes talent mapping and workforce analytics capabilities. It helps organizations identify internal talent, assess skill gaps, and plan for future workforce needs.

These tools use data analytics, artificial intelligence, and machine learning to provide valuable insights into the talent market. They help organizations make informed decisions about talent acquisition, workforce planning, and overall human resource strategies.

CANDIDATE REFERENCES

Candidates you are already engaged with might know individuals suitable for the position. Do not hesitate to ask them for references. They might know professionals who are actively seeking new opportunities.

There are some tools for candidate reference which not only help in checking a candidate's background but some of them provide database access to their connections who are added as references. Once the references opt-in to stay updated with the company positions and updates, they can be considered for future openings.

EMPLOYEE REFERRALS

You need to encourage current employees to refer candidates. They can vouch for the company's culture and work environment, making the opportunity more appealing to their connections. In the coming chapter, you will find a detailed description of the Employee Referral Program.

While we implement these tools, it is important for organizations to consider their specific needs, the nature of the positions they are hiring for, and any compliance requirements. In fact, integration with existing HR systems and applicant tracking systems can enhance the overall efficiency of the hiring process.

All we need to ensure is that the selected tools are aligned with our organization's policies and legal requirements for all kinds of data privacy.

LET'S SYNTHESIZE

What are your top 3 preferred sourcing and attraction tools for recruitment?

....
....
....
....
....

What features do you like the most in those tools and why?

....
....
....
....
....

If traditional job portals which provide resume searching capabilities and job search capabilities are taken away from you, including all kinds of paid subscriptions, and you are given the task of sourcing only from the open web and social media channels, what would your approach be?

....
....
....
....

Like Data Scientists can be found on Kaggle, what other tools can you target to find candidates of a specific skill set?

....

....

....

....

....

8

BUILDING A STRONGER
TEAM TOGETHER: POWER OF REFERRALS

Imagine being able to help your company find the perfect new team member. Just like recommending a fantastic new restaurant to a friend, suggesting a great person for a job at your company can make the process smoother and more reliable. Your insights and recommendations can become the key to unlocking the best talent for your workplace.

WHY REFERRALS WORK WONDERS?

Employee Referrals are like trusted recommendations or endorsements. When you are referring someone, you are vouching for their skills, abilities, work ethic, and overall fitment for the company.

A WIN-WIN SITUATION

When you refer someone, not only are you showing trust and favouring a person you know professionally or personally, but you are also eligible for awards and recognition if your referral gets selected and joins your organization.

Companies follow different methods of rewarding employees for providing good referrals. These could be in the form of extra money, customized gifts, gift vouchers, or expensive utility gifts. It is a way to express gratitude that goes a long way in building a strong and supportive workplace culture.

This is a win-win situation for referees, referrals, and the organization. An employee referral gets someone a job, the employee gets the reward, and the company gets an engaged hire whose possibility of joining is higher than a regular candidate.

EMBRACING DIVERSITY IN EMPLOYEE REFERRAL PROGRAMS

It is a known fact that every workplace thrives on diversity and every person brings something unique to the table. When suggesting potential candidates, keep in mind that it is important for any organization to have different perspectives and experiences. Someone who speaks a different language or comes from a different background could bring in fresh ideas and make your workplace even more culturally diverse. Even employees coming from different geographical and educational backgrounds add a lot of value to the diversity of the organization.

KEY STRATEGIES FOR A SUCCESSFUL REFERRAL PROGRAM

To implement an effective employee referral program, consider the following practical strategies:

Share Open Positions through Internal Communication: We need to ensure that everyone clearly understands the program's objectives and guidelines through regular communication and updates. The talent acquisition team should send regular updates to all the employees regarding current open positions.

This will enable employees to leverage their own professional and personal network and refer candidates who they think are suitable for the role. So, as the first step, all the open positions should be posted internally so that employees can refer their friends and acquaintances.

Offer Awards/Incentives: This is another important parameter of a strong employee referral program. The stronger the incentive or reward system of the employee referral program, the larger the talent pool we receive through employee referral campaigns.

User-friendly Process: The referral method should be kept simple in terms of providing an easy platform to upload or share referrals. If this process is tedious, employees will try to reach out to recruiters or sourcers directly to refer to their profiles which makes it difficult to track them and keep a record.

Regular Updates on Referred Candidates: Keep employees engaged by providing regular updates on the employee referral program's progress and success stories. Transparent feedback to employees about their referrals helps them refer even more relevant candidates in future as per the positions.

Regular Training and Support: Provide regular training and guidance to employees on identifying potential candidates through their professional networks, improving their understanding of the job description and referring to the candidates effectively.

Encourage Diversity: Encourage diversity by urging employees to refer candidates from various backgrounds and experiences. You can introduce additional incentives for referring and helping candidates from various diverse groups join the organization.

Appreciation and Recognition: Recognize and appreciate employees who actively participate in the referral program to encourage ongoing engagement. This can be done through gamifying employee referral programs and providing additional awards to the top referees.

My previous company used to conduct a gamification event for this program for a certain duration of the year where they used to run different campaigns to encourage employees to refer more candidates. The top three referees in the entire game season used to get some attractive awards, and this was in addition to the regular employee referral bounties.

Feedback and Improvement: Create a feedback mechanism to gather insights and continuously improve the referral program's effectiveness and inclusivity.

By integrating these practices, many companies have already been able to establish strong employee referral programs that not only attract top talent but also nurture a strong, diverse and engaging workplace culture.

"People Influence people. A trusted referral influences people more than the best broadcast message. A trusted referral is the Holy Grail of advertising."

– Mark Zuckerberg

LET'S SYNTHESIZE

What innovative ways can you think of for incentivizing employees to provide referrals? Can you specify any two?

....

....

....

....

....

Have you come across any challenges or foresee any challenges in your existing employee referral program? How do you think those challenges can be addressed?

....

....

....

....

....

What does a successful employee referral program mean to you?

....

....

....

....

9

THE PASSIVE TALENT POOL

Passive candidates should be treated differently from active ones since they are individuals whom you reach out to for their unique skills and experience and invite to apply for a job opportunity. It is important to treat them with the same level of attention and respect that you would give to a specially invited guest for whom you go the extra mile to make them feel welcome and valued.

Before we talk about the passive talent pool, it is important to understand what being active means in recruitment. Normally, we all understand being active as being prompt, responsive and alert.

In recruitment, reaching out to active candidates is easy as they are the ones who are looking for a job change, they are the ones who are highly active in the market and their resumes are always up to date. When we post any jobs, they are the ones who apply without any delay.

The only limitation of targeting active candidates is the risk of losing them to the market. When they apply to your jobs, they are also applying to other companies, and they end up joining the one which gives them more flexibility, better opportunities, and more benefits.

Considering the uncertainty around these candidates joining the company, it's always recommended to target the passive talent pool.

Passive talent pool refers to a group of people who are currently employed and not actively searching for a job, but who may still be interested in hearing about new job opportunities. These candidates have skills, experience, and knowledge that may be valuable to potential employers, but they are not necessarily actively looking to make a career move now.

You may have encountered passive talent without even realizing it. For example, you may have a friend or acquaintance who is currently employed, but who would be a great fit for a job opening about which you have heard of. This person may not be actively searching for a job, but if you can present the opportunity in a compelling way, they may be interested in learning more.

From an employer's perspective, the passive talent pool can be a valuable resource for finding top talent. Instead of relying solely on job postings and active job seekers, employers can identify individuals who have the skills and experience they need and reach out to them directly to gauge their interest in a job opportunity.

To have them apply to your positions, you need to follow different talent attraction strategies. You need to target different passive platforms like Github, Kaggle, Dribbble, Behance, etc. where they have their professional profiles and professional portfolios updated.

When you reach out to them, let them know that you have visited their profile and reviewed their work and you are impressed by the projects they have executed. Introduce yourself and your organization and let them know that you have reached out to them to offer an opportunity which might be suitable for them.

You need to treat passive candidates differently as they are the ones you reached out to and invited to apply for your jobs, the way you treat your special invited guests.

I still remember my first ever experience of sourcing from a passive sourcing platform. This was in 2015 when I was asked to find a visual designer with the specific requirement of certain skills and portfolios. I explored regular job portals where I could just find the description of the projects and designs, but it was difficult to review their work on the basis of a few website links they had given. I had to review the same profile on multiple platforms to validate the designer's work.

Later, I gave up on the regular platforms after multiple screen rejections and explored Behance; it is a platform where designers not only create their professional profiles, but they maintain their portfolios. This platform is designed to showcase all their design-related work. I reviewed a couple of profiles and reached out to a few candidates. To my surprise, out of three candidates we finally shortlisted, one of them cleared the interview and was offered the role.

I understood that if you need to find some good talent, you cannot just rely on one or two platforms, but also go through their work displayed in various places.

Here are some examples of platforms tailored to specific industries or roles that can be effective for finding passive candidates:

❖ **Behance:** As mentioned above, this platform is dedicated to showcasing creative portfolios, making it ideal for sourcing graphic designers, illustrators, and other visual artists.

❖ **GitHub:** A hub for developers, GitHub allows professionals to showcase their coding skills, projects, and contributions. It is an excellent platform for sourcing software developers, programmers, and other tech-related roles.

❖ **Dribbble:** Like Behance, Dribbble focuses on design professionals, especially those involved in web and app design, UI/UX, and other digital design roles.

❖ **Kaggle:** Specifically designed for data scientists and machine learning practitioners, Kaggle hosts competitions and allows data scientists to showcase their skills and projects.

❖ **AngelList:** Primarily catering to startups and tech companies, AngelList is a great platform to find tech talent, including developers.

❖ **Quora:** Though it is a platform to ask questions and get answers from experts, some sourcers track experts specific to the skills they are hiring for and try reaching out to them for those positions.

I once read an interesting quote about recruiters:

WE ARE PROFESSIONAL STALKERS BUT IN A TOTALLY LEGAL WAY.

LET'S SYNTHESIZE

When you already know that passive talent may not be actively looking for a job change, why do you think they could be still important to an organization? Why would you still think of targeting them?

....

....

....

....

How can you build a strong relationship with potential passive candidates as a recruiter?

....

....

....

....

What strategy would you follow to find passive candidates considering that they are not easily available or cannot be easily sourced through traditional job boards?

....

....

....

....

....

10

SEARCHING TECHNIQUES
AND BOOLEAN LOGIC

Every time I offer a prayer to God, I try to be very precise in terms of my choices, my wishes and what I want. I also clearly specify the things I want to stay away from.

First of all, let me define Boolean for you, it is a logic used in data, driven by computer science where any value can be either true or false with true being one and false being zero. Boolean gets its name from the mathematician George Boole who created the Boolean algebraic formula.

Now, you must be wondering why I am discussing math, logic, and algebra here when we are talking about sourcing and searching.

Basically, there are two different methods of sourcing and searching for candidates. We can either go for a regular keyword search the way we do Google searches or shop from e-commerce websites. The other method to search for a perfect fit is using Boolean operators to create your search strings.

If you are already into recruitment, I am sure you must be aware of keyword search techniques but if you are new to the industry and need some training or a refresher on this, here you go:

KEYWORD SEARCH

Keyword searches are a fundamental aspect of job board and recruitment platform functionality. They allow recruiters and job seekers to find relevant job listings or candidates by entering specific keywords or phrases. These searches help users narrow down their options and save time by displaying results that match their criteria. Here are the parameters and examples of advanced keyword searches on popular job boards including LinkedIn Recruiter.

Keywords: This is where you enter the terms related to the job or the candidate you are looking for like the skills or programming language or good communication skills, etc.

Location: Specify the geographical location where you want to find candidates or jobs. It could be the candidate's current location or preferred locations based on the job locations. For example, if the role is based in Hyderabad, you can specify the current location: Hyderabad or the preferred location: Hyderabad. For remote roles, you can select multiple target locations as per pool availability.

Industry: Filter results by industry or sector like Information Technology, Telecommunication, etc.

Company: Search with specific company names for targeted search results. This could be based on the talent insights and availability of the talent on the top five or ten companies.

Job Title: Search for candidates with specific job titles like Full Stack Developer, Social Media Manager, etc.

School: Look for candidates from educational institutions.

Experience Range: Look for candidates within a specific experience range. For example, if you are hiring for a mid-senior level you can specify an experience range from five to eight years or eight to ten years depending on the experience requirement of the role.

BOOLEAN LOGIC

When I was studying logic gates like AND, OR NOT, I never realized I would be utilizing this logic so much in my day-to-day life.

Every time I offer a prayer to God, I try to be very precise in terms of my choices and wishes and clearly specify the things I want to stay away from. I do this because I do not want to create any confusion about my choices and the things I want to eliminate from my life. Similarly, I am very careful while searching for candidates on job portals or on social media through advanced or detailed searches.

The best way to become as accurate in our searches as we are in our choices is to go Boolean. I have realized that Boolean could be the new synonym for being accurate. In simple words, Boolean search is a search technique that allows you to combine keywords and phrases using operators such as 'AND', 'OR' and 'NOT'. By using these operators, you can refine your search and retrieve more accurate and relevant results.

- ❖ Boolean Operators:
  - ✦ AND

- ✦ OR
- ✦ NOT
- ❖ Boolean Modifiers
  - ✦ Asterisk *
  - ✦ Parentheses ()
  - ✦ Quotation Marks " "
- ❖ **AND:** Used to narrow the search

  Example: Happiness AND Love AND Health AND Wealth AND Satisfaction
- ❖ **OR:** Used to broaden the search

  Example: Friends **OR** Family **OR** (Friends AND Family)
- ❖ **NOT:** Not is used to eliminate the word

  Example: Everything NOT Sadness
- ❖ **- (Minus) Sign** can be used as a NOT operator in Google and LinkedIn search
- ❖ **"": Inverted Commas** are used to restrict the search for more than one Keyword.

  Example: "Successful Business" OR "Highly Paid Job"
- ❖ **Parenthesis ():** Used to categorize keywords.

  Example: Friends OR Family OR (Friends AND Family)
- ❖ *** (Asterisk)** used as a root word search.

  Example: Config* = (configure OR configuring OR configured OR configures)

BOOLEAN OPERATOR VS LIFE OBJECTIVES

Now if I am looking for a life filled with happiness, love, health, wealth, and satisfaction; where there should be no space for sadness, hatred, competition tears; where I should be staying with my family and my friends and I should either own a successful business or should have a good job. I have a Boolean form of the above statement.

Life **AND** Happiness **AND** Love **AND** Health **AND** Wealth **AND** Satisfaction

AND Family **AND** Friends **AND** ("Successful Business" **OR** "Good Job")

NOT Sadness **NOT** Hatred **NOT** Competition **NOT** Tears

I have conducted many training sessions on different topics of recruitment and one of my favourites is Boolean search. As my most preferred activity after every session, I always provide a task to all the training attendees. I tell them to define themselves in a Boolean string. All they need to do is consider the list of their qualities, strengths, weaknesses, and habits they want to get rid of. Their Boolean string should be the method for them to introduce themselves.

Another assignment I give them is to make a professional Boolean string which will help me find them on Google without using their names. It is a fun activity; I am sure you would also like to try this once.

Once you know how to play around with Boolean logic, you would prefer to use this for your candidate search and will get relevant results. The best practice to follow as soon as you get a job description is to identify all important keywords, put them together and go Boolean!

XRAY SEARCH

Xray search is an effective tool for targeting the passive talent pool. It is a technique that uses specific search phrases to find potential candidates or relevant information on the internet. These search phrases, called Xray search operators, help to narrow down the search results to a specific website, keyword, or type of content. Using Xray search is helpful because it can uncover information or candidates that may not be easily found on traditional job sites or databases. However, it requires some technical knowledge to be used effectively.

XRAY-SEARCH OPERATORS:

- ❖ Colon:
- ❖ Brackets ()
- ❖ Boolean Operators
- ❖ Minus –
- ❖ Site: (Site Colon) It Xray the site
- ❖ Filetype: (Filetype Colon) It x-rays the document.
- ❖ Intitle: (Intitle Colon) It x-rays the title.

Few Examples of Xray passive platforms:

- ❖ **Xray Google:** intitle: resume OR inurl: resume (Java AND Developer AND "United States") -job -jobs -sample -samples -template -" resumes services" - "resume writer" -"resume writing"
- ❖ filetype:doc OR filetype:pdf (intitle: resume OR inurl: resume) (WordPress AND PHP AND mysql AND "United States")

- ❖ **Xray Behance: site:** behance.net (Visual AND Designer AND "Germany" AND "On Behance") -"Work Experience" -"Creative jobs" -Agencies -"Search users"

- ❖ **Xray Dribbble: site:** dribbble.com (California AND "Graphic Designer") AND "Member since"

- ❖ **Xray Kaggle: Site:** Kaggle.com "Last Seen" ("United States" AND "Data Science" AND California)

- ❖ **Xray Quora:** site: quora.com/profile "lives * Pune" "Dentist"

- ❖ **Xray Stackover Flow:**

    site: careers.stackoverflow.com ((Python) AND "United States") -jobs -inurl:company

LET'S SYNTHESIZE

Frame a Boolean string for yourself without putting your name and last two organization names. Can you still find your own profile as a search result of your string?

....

....

....

....

Can you define your interests, hobbies, likes, and dislikes in the form of a Boolean string which can utilize all the Boolean operators?

....

....

....

....

Take any job description and run two different searches, one with Boolean string and one without and review the accuracy of the profiles displayed in the results. What is your analysis?

....

....

....

....

....

11
ATTRACTING AND HIRING
A DIVERSE TALENT POOL

Imagine you are planning a potluck dinner, and everyone brings the same dish. It might taste good, but it lacks variety. Now, think of a diverse potluck where each person brings a unique dish. It becomes a more vibrant and flavourful experience, offering different tastes.

In the same way, diversity in people brings a variety of ideas, skills, and viewpoints, making our communities and workplaces richer and more successful.

Giving importance to diversity in the workplace is an essential aspect of any successful organization. A diverse talent pool brings a range of perspectives, experiences, and skills that can drive innovation at the workplace, improve decision-making and enhance overall performance.

In this chapter, I would like to take you through the importance of attracting and hiring a diverse talent pool along with numerous examples of how to do that.

DEFINING DIVERSITY

Diversity consists of various factors, including gender, race, ethnicity, age, sexual orientation, physical abilities, and more.

Encouraging diversity in the workplace simply indicates that we encourage differences.

DEFINING INCLUSION

Valuing diversity in the workplace is inclusion. When all the team members are given equal opportunities based on their roles and experience, when all of them are heard, respected, engaged and trained equally irrespective of their background, and when they feel a sense of belonging, we can say that the organization has an inclusive culture.

In many organizations, diversity is encouraged to meet compliance or to meet a target; however, I strongly believe that a strong recruitment team would organically hire a diverse talent pool with different skills and from varying backgrounds.

Diversity hiring should happen naturally as a part of the recruiting process, however, it also requires additional efforts which leads to advantages associated with hiring diverse talent pools which keep the organizations motivated.

DEFINING EQUITY AND EQUALITY

We often hear about organizations calling themselves equal-opportunity employers. When the employees know that there is no biased behaviour in the organization, and they are treated like their peers, they feel safe and valued.

Providing equality appears to be a requirement but only providing it may not be practical unless we consider equity.

Equality is about giving similar resources to everyone irrespective of their experience, expertise, and knowledge.

Equity is about considering the background of the employees and accordingly providing specific resources to them based on their needs to help them achieve their goals.

For example, in a team of five recruiters, two might be good at volume hiring which requires general skills, two at niche hiring which requires very rare or difficult-to-find skills and one at leadership hiring. Giving all of them a project which focuses on leadership hiring without giving them specific training may lead to an increased turnaround time for finding candidates. Instead, we should be providing additional training to four team members who have limited exposure to leadership hiring.

WHY DEIB?

I would like to share with you some rationale on why we need diversity, equity, and inclusion in the workplace. Many industry experts talk about the core reasons in different ways, but the sole purpose remains the same everywhere.

❖ **Encourages Creativity and Innovation:** Undoubtedly, a diverse team can offer different methods of executing and implementing projects through diverse ideas and approaches. When we have team members from different backgrounds and they collaborate with each other, they can generate quite innovative and creative solutions to complex problems.

❖ **Improved Decision-Making:** Diverse teams are more likely to make better decisions because they can consider different perspectives on different situations from their own experiences and are able to proactively identify bottlenecks and opportunities.

❖ **Better Employee Engagement and Retention:** A diverse and inclusive team encourages a sense of responsibility and ownership among employees, which results in better employee engagement and retention. An organization which has a non-diverse leadership may never be able to relate to the challenges the team is facing and may not be able to offer valuable solutions.

❖ **Legal and Ethical Compliance:** Many countries or regions have rules/laws and regulations which are meant to encourage and promote diversity and inclusion. Since they are bound by law, any sort of non-compliance leads to legal issues and may damage the reputation of the organization.

I would like to share some references which exemplify rules and regulations towards promoting diversity and inclusion.

The U.S. Department of Labor has clearly specified the following on its website:

At the Office of Federal Contract Compliance Programs (OFCCP), we protect workers, promote diversity and enforce the law. OFCCP holds those who do business with the federal government (contractors and subcontractors) responsible for complying with the legal requirement to take affirmative action and not discriminate based on race, colour, sex, sexual orientation, gender identity, religion, national origin, disability, or status as a protected veteran. In addition, contractors, and subcontractors are prohibited from discharging or otherwise discriminating against applicants or employees who inquire about, discuss or disclose their compensation or that of others, subject to certain limitations.

Source: https://www.dol.gov/agencies/ofccp/about

Disability:In has specified the following on their website (Homepage - Disability:IN (disabilityin.org)

Companies in Brazil need to meet a hiring quota for persons with disabilities that ranges from two per cent to five per cent depending on company size:

Fewer than one hundred employees	*no requirement*
00 to 200 employees	*2 per cent*
201 to 500 employees	*3 per cent*
501 to 1000 employees	*4 per cent*
Over one thousand employees	*5 per cent*

You can learn more from the source: https://disabilityin.org/country/brazil/

PRACTICAL STRATEGIES FOR ATTRACTING AND HIRING DIVERSE TALENT

Now, let us explore some methods to attract and hire a diverse talent pool:

❖ **Inclusive Job Postings:** We need to use inclusive language in job descriptions and postings to encourage candidates from all backgrounds to apply.

❖ **Diverse Sourcing Channels:** We need to cast a wide net when sourcing candidates. As a best practice, we need to utilize all available job boards, leverage their diversity filters, attend networking events, and partner with diversity-focused organizations to reach a broader audience.

❖ **Structured Interviews:** Implement structured interviews with standardized questions to reduce biases during the hiring process. During interviews, ask candidates to provide specific examples of their skills and experiences which can help them bring their diverse perspectives to the table.

❖ **Diversity Training:** It is important to organize diversity and inclusion-specific training for recruiters, hiring managers and employees to adopt a more inclusive workplace culture.

❖ **Create and Leverage Employee Resource Groups (ERG):** The presence of ERGs in organizations can help employees feel more included in the workplace. ERGs are formed with employees of shared identities and backgrounds. ERGs can be formed with groups of veterans, women or can be based on physical abilities/ disability, ethnicity, etc.

Attracting and hiring a diverse talent pool is not just a moral obligation; it is a deliberate advantage that can drive an organization's success in today's diverse and interconnected world.

Here is a list of tools that can be used to source a diverse talent pool:

1. **Diversity-Focused Job Boards:** There are multiple job boards which provide filters to source from a diverse talent pool. Additionally, there are many job boards which only provide access to a diverse pool. Sharing a few examples here:

   ✦ **DiversityJobs/Women in Tech**: Women in Tech is an international organization on a mission to close the gender gap and to help women embrace technology.

✦ **Black Career Network:** A job board which helps employers to connect with diverse talent through job postings.

✦ **HireEz:** HireEz provides search filters which can help source candidates based on gender, colour, region, etc.

✦ **MitraTech's Circa:** Circa helps expand the organization's reach to the database of all local job boards of the United States, helps manage job distribution to state job banks and veteran organizations, provides automatic and targeted outreach to 15k + community-based organizations and helps manage applicant workflow.

2. **Social Media Platforms:** Like regular sourcing, we can utilize the platforms below to source diverse talent.

✦ **LinkedIn:** You can join and leverage different diversity groups and connect with diverse talent pools.

✦ **X:** Through X, we can engage with diverse communities through tweets using relevant hashtags and skills.

✦ **Facebook:** You can join or create groups focused on diversity in specific industries. There are many existing groups on Facebook which have a good database of active candidates.

3. **Networking Events Platforms**

✦ **LGBTQ Pride Summit:** There are many networking groups which organize conferences or events focussed on inviting speakers and delegates from diverse groups. LGBTQ pride summit promotes self-affirmation, dignity, equality and increased visibility of lesbian, gay, bisexual, and transgender people as social groups.

+ **NAAAP Leadership Convention:** This is the largest event of the year organized by the National Association of Asian American Professionals. This convention is a time to hear inspirational speakers and learn about corporate practices in diversity and talent management, emerging topics and best practices, make new friends and renew old friendships, and recognize Asian leaders at every level – lifetime contributors, community unsung heroes, and NAAAP leaders. Source: https://boston.naaap.org/events/naaap-national-leadership-convention

+ **Employee Referral Programs:** We can encourage employees to refer diverse talent from their network for open positions.

+ **University Hiring:** We can target institutes/universities for campus placements which have students from diverse groups. For example, many companies give their initial slots of hiring to women. There are companies which identify institutes to hire candidates with different disabilities.

+ **AI-Based Recruitment Tools:** We can use many tools and platforms which help us create a more inclusive hiring process to target a diverse talent pool.

+ **Textio:** It helps analyze job descriptions and emails and suggests improvements to make content more inclusive.

+ **GapJumpers:** They offer tools to eliminate bias from sourcing and hiring and help in designing bias-free processes.

+ **Company Diversity and Inclusion Pages:** Every company should have a dedicated section or tab within the careers page which can showcase the company's value and culture, which emphasizes its inclination towards DEIB.

+ **Collaboration with Diversity Organizations:** There are many organizations like the National Society of Black Engineers or Out & Equal which can help in accessing diverse talent pools. You can find several such organizations or groups in LinkedIn groups.

LET'S SYNTHESIZE

Think of a team with people of similar gender, background, location, and education; what challenges do you think that team can face and how can this be reversed by hiring diversity in all these categories?

....

....

....

....

....

If you are given the responsibility to take initiative with respect to hiring practices which are inclusive and bias-free, what would your first three steps be?

....

....

....

....

....

12

TALENT ATTRACTION AND RECRUITMENT MARKETING

We now know that attracting candidates is no longer about creating a push strategy by reaching out to them, but it is more about generating a pull strategy and making them interested in our positions.

We talked about the four important pillars of the recruitment life cycle which are attract, connect, engage and experience and this continues from attracting candidates to onboarding them.

In this chapter, we will take some time to understand the first stage – talent attraction. There was a time when recruiters used to call candidates once they figured out that their profiles could be fit for the role, but it is no longer considered an ideal practice. Recruiters now prefer reaching out to candidates with a proposal of the offer they have for them and only if the candidate expresses interest, they reach out to them considering the candidate's availability and preferred method of communication.

We now know that attracting candidates is no longer about creating a push strategy by reaching out to them, but it is more about generating a pull strategy and making them interested in our positions.

I remember, as a child, the first few items which I picked from the market were the ones I had seen the most on television. Be it my favourite cookies or beverages, I loved to pick up those which looked familiar to me. I expressed interest in trying them as I was already a big fan of the way they were advertised and had been able to already establish a connection with me. The case of recruitment is no different. The basic law of attracting candidates starts with establishing a strong brand-generating recall.

'Talent attraction' and 'recruitment marketing' sound like different terms though they both are connected to each other in the context of talent acquisition. I would like to take you through this in a little more detail.

TALENT ATTRACTION

Talent attraction, as the name itself suggests, refers to the process of drawing top-quality candidates to your organization. It involves creating a very appealing employer brand, creating and maintaining a strong online presence on all suitable platforms including social media channels, job boards, review platforms, networking events and targeting specific talent pools to fill our job openings.

Major components of talent attraction are listed below but are not just limited to these:

- ❖ **Employer Branding:** it is well known that building a positive image of your company as an employer is crucial. It involves showcasing your organization's culture, values, and benefits to prospective candidates.

Many leading organizations are renowned for their appealing employer brand. Few of them offer unique rewards like free meals, flexible work hours, and an inclusive and fun-filled work environment.

❖ **Strong Online Presence:** A strong online presence is extremely critical for attracting talent nowadays. This includes maintaining an engaging and user-friendly website, active and lively social media profiles, and active participation in relevant online communities. Most of the companies now regularly share employee stories and company culture content on their blog and social media channels.

❖ **Targeted Outreach:** Rather than casting a wide net, focussing your efforts on reaching out to specific talent pools work better. For example, if you are looking for software developers, you may consider organizing or sponsoring coding events like hackathons, tech fests, tech conferences or may encourage your talent acquisition team and employees to actively attend these events or hackathons.

RECRUITMENT MARKETING

Recruitment marketing is a subset of talent attraction that involves using marketing strategies to nurture and engage potential candidates. It is about treating candidates like customers and guiding them through a structured recruitment process.

Recruitment Marketing has following key components:

❖ **Content Marketing:** You need to create informative and engaging content that can provide useful information to candidates about the company, industry, and job opportunities.

Companies use taglines or hashtags to market their brand and content together. Example #Weareviasat, #lifeatcapgemini, 'Once an Infoscion, Always an Infoscion'

❖ **Email Marketing:** We need to generate email campaigns and automate the emailing process through customized templates to stay in touch with candidates. It is important to share updates about the organization, relevant job openings, and content that provides value to candidates.

Companies send personalized emails to candidates based on their preferences and interactions with the company's career website.

❖ **Candidate Relationship Management (CRM):** It is a good practice to implement a Candidate Relationship Management tool which can either be a part of your applicant tracking system or can be integrated to the same to manage candidate interactions and track the journey of candidates.

This way companies and their recruiters can provide a more personalized experience to candidates by staying in touch with them and sharing timely feedback.

❖ **Social Media Advertising:** We need to leverage social media platforms like LinkedIn, Facebook, and X to target specific candidate demographics with job ads. Many global tech giants are effectively using LinkedIn organic campaigns or sponsored content to promote their job openings to a targeted audience.

❖ **Onboard External Agencies:** Many companies outsource their recruitment marketing to external agencies to create and manage campaigns; however, this needs strong coordination between the external agency and the internal team. For external agencies to be able to execute the campaigns successfully, they are provided with the details of candidates whom companies would like to target based on their historical hiring trends.

We will talk more about candidate persona in a later chapter.

❖ **Set Examples and Precedences:** Many employers set examples within their industry on providing world class employee and candidate experience and this, in turn, helps them get established as a strong employer brand. I often receive emails from my previous employers on latest updates and open opportunities. It is an effective way to keep me engaged and generate a recall value. This approach also creates a sense of belonging among ex-employees.

There are companies which customize their communication based on the candidate's area of interest. If a candidate is a guitar player, he/she may also receive updates regarding such musical events happening in the company which keeps the candidate engaged and interested.

There are many companies who encourage diversity in the workplace, and they happily extend offers to pregnant women who are soon going to be on a maternity break. This reflects the inclusive and bias-free culture of organizations.

❖ **Employee Advocacy:** Employee Advocacy in recruitment marketing refers to active involvement and support by current employees to promote their company in a more natural and organic way as the employer of their choice. It is similar to word-of-mouth publicity of any product or brand. Employees share their day-to-day stories, talk about positive aspects of their work life and the sense of pride they feel about working with their organization.

Through employee advocacy, we can leverage the professional network of current employees which helps amplify the brand value of the organization resulting in attracting potential candidates. There are tools to facilitate employee advocacy, to enable them to voice their experience and share their stories or like and comment on other stories in a convenient way.

Talent attraction and recruitment marketing are crucial for attracting and retaining top talent. By adopting these strategies and leveraging digital tools, companies can create a compelling employer brand, engage with potential candidates and build a strong and diverse workforce. These examples demonstrate how leading organizations effectively implement these concepts to meet their talent acquisition goals.

"Recruitment is Marketing. If you are a recruiter nowadays and you do not see yourself as a marketer, you are in the wrong profession."

– Mathew Jeffery

LET'S SYNTHESIZE

Design your recruitment marketing strategy.

....

....

....

....

....

As per you, how can organizations measure the return on investment of recruitment marketing initiatives?

....

....

....

....

....

13
CAMPUS RECRUITMENT

Many organizations prefer hiring early graduates over experienced people for a high volume of positions which require trainable skills. Early graduates bring new ideas, enthusiasm, and innovative solutions to the workplace. Based on their degrees and specializations and the projects they have undergone during their internships, they may also possess knowledge of the latest skills and technology.

Although experienced professionals bring their work experience, skills and knowledge to the workplace which might not be the case with early graduates but when it comes to hiring in volume and for regular skills, the latter are the preferred choice of many organizations.

I would like to share an overview of how companies approach campus hiring through the following steps:

1. **Identifying universities or colleges:** As a first step, companies first identify the universities or colleges they want to target for campus recruitment based on factors like institution's ranking, course curriculum and student demographics.

2. **Pre-placement talks:** Before the placement drive, companies schedule pre-placement talks or webinars

where they introduce their organization, work culture and the job roles available. These talks are very crucial as they help build employer branding and create awareness among the students about the company. This is the time when students make up their minds about which company they would prefer.

3. **Job posting and application:** Companies also post job openings on career portals of institutions or through campus placement offices. Interested students then apply for the openings by submitting their resumes, cover letters, or application forms.

4. **Short-listing:** Based on the applications received, companies shortlist students who meet their eligibility and qualification criteria. They may also conduct an initial screening to filter out unsuitable candidates. Many companies set some benchmarks on the basis of minimum percentage required in Grades 10 and 12 which become the initial screening criteria for a resume to move forward.

5. **Campus visit:** Most of the companies follow the campus calendar for scheduled recruitment drives. Once the campus is identified, pre-placement talks are organized and resumes are shortlisted, companies visit the college campus on a scheduled date for the recruitment drive. Recruitment drives mostly include written tests, group discussions, technical and behavioural interviews, and other assessments to evaluate the candidates' suitability for the role.

6. **Final selection:** Once the final shortlisting of students is done, companies extend job offers to the selected

candidates. The candidates are presented with offer letters, salary details, benefits, and other information.

7. **Onboarding:** Like the regular onboarding, once the students from campus accept the offer, they are required to undergo a period of induction, training, and onboarding to get familiar with the company culture, policies, and work.

8. **Technical training:** Many companies put campus hires on a skill-based training plan where they are trained in batches on different skills. This helps companies to allocate training resources to different projects.

Other than on-campus hiring, companies also hire fresh talent through off-campus drives and other tools and platforms.

OFF-CAMPUS RECRUITMENT DRIVES

In the year 2006, I was placed in Infosys through an off-campus drive. The recruitment process for off-campus drives is similar to the on-campus one except for the application process where students across different colleges can apply instead of just one college where the company is visiting. Based on the shortlisting of their profiles, companies visit the college which has been identified for the drive.

Since the number of applications are likely to be higher than the regular campus drives, many companies follow an elimination process where they shortlist applications based on academic scores, high cut off during written exams, group screening before the interview process, etc.

The rest of the process of extending the offer, onboarding and training remains very similar to the on-campus interviews.

The most important part of campus placement is to identify colleges and there are different ways of doing the same:

❖ **Internships:** Companies can identify potential campuses for recruitment by offering internships to students from selected universities or colleges. This can help in building relationships with the institution and provide the opportunity to evaluate students' performance, competencies, and other desirable traits which can be useful in the full-time recruitment process.

❖ **Recruitment Webinars:** Companies can host online webinars, go live through LinkedIn or conduct in-person sessions very similar to pre-placement talks to provide insights on their organizations, job roles, and other relevant information to students. This can help in attracting and engaging potential candidates and build brand awareness.

❖ **Hackathons:** Hackathons are events where students come together to find solutions for technical challenges or problems related to day-to-day life using technology or

> CAMPUS RECRUITMENT IS CONSIDERED ONE OF THE MOST PREFERRED WAYS OF HIRING TALENT WHEN IT COMES TO FILLING DEMANDS WHICH ARE HIGH IN VOLUME AND NEED FRESH GRADUATES WITH THE RIGHT ATTITUDE, EAGERNESS TO LEARN AND WILLINGNESS TO APPLY THEIR LEARNING AT THE WORKPLACE.

innovative solutions. Companies can sponsor these events or organize hackathons themselves, which can help in identifying talented students, increase brand visibility and build long-term relationships with universities or colleges.

❖ **Online Skill Assessments:** Companies can use skill assessment platforms such as Hacker Rank and other similar tools to filter out students based on their technical skills and knowledge of relevant technologies.

❖ **Tools and Software:** Platforms like Handshake, Symplicity, GradLeaders, Yello, 12Twenty, etc., can help companies identify potential colleges or universities, narrow down the target audience and manage the recruitment process more efficiently. They also provide a channel for companies to connect with students seeking internships or job opportunities.

Campus recruitment is considered one of the most preferred ways of hiring talent when it comes to filling demands which are high in volume and need fresh graduates with the right attitude, eagerness to learn and willingness to apply their learning at the workplace. Companies can effectively run campus programs if they have the right strategy to conduct campus interviews and an effective learning and development function to run the training program.

LET'S SYNTHESIZE

If you are assigned a task of recruiting two hundred candidates who would be deployed for six to eight months in a live project, what would be your approach?

....

....

....

....

....

What should be some important parameters for a company to identify the colleges they need to visit in their next placement season?

....

....

....

....

....

14

DEFINING CANDIDATE PERSONAS

If the personas are not defined, any kind of advertisement may not be relevant and may not yield any results.

Candidate personas in recruitment marketing are like detailed charts outlining the characteristics of the perfect candidates for a specific job role. They can be as detailed as a personalized profile that includes details about a candidate's background, motivations, challenges, and even their online presence. In simple words, a candidate persona delineates specific skills and qualities for a particular kind of professional group e.g., software developers, visual designers, sales representatives, etc.

These personas help recruiters and marketers design their messages to attract the right people for the job. It is like speaking directly to your ideal candidates, making your recruitment efforts more effective and engaging.

As I mentioned in one of the previous chapters, many companies utilize external agencies for their recruitment marketing efforts. If your organization decides to advertise a few job roles, the first step would be to define the audience and their interest.

If you are a job seeker and you keep seeing the job of a sales manager on a continuous basis which is a paid promotion of a job, do you think it will ever make you apply for the job role even if you see it multiple times? If the personas are not defined, any kind of advertisement may not be relevant and may not yield any results.

It always makes sense to identify personas before you advertise your roles on different platforms.

Steps to define candidate personas:

❖ Identify the desired qualities of a perfect candidate.

❖ Understand all platforms where your ideal candidate can exist.

❖ Understand your ideal candidate's aspirations in terms of company culture, job titles, projects, work-life balance, etc.

❖ Analyze historical data to capture important insights on similar branding activity.

❖ Create a strategy for recruitment marketing.

HOW TO COLLECT DETAILED INSIGHTS

❖ Ask relevant questions to candidates and record them in the system.

❖ Explore their LinkedIn profiles.

❖ Conduct surveys within different segments of candidates and collect their responses on how they secured the job, what do they like best about their company, USPs, etc.

Information you should collect from candidates/employees to design persona-driven recruitment marketing:

❖ **Job Search Preferences:** Preferred application method/communication method, preferred job platforms etc. For example, few candidates prefer applying on a career website directly however few prefer applying through LinkedIn or other job boards.

❖ **Professional Details:** Current role/skills/goals, etc. which can lead to interpretations. For example, like candidates with the role of a data analyst with knowledge of SQL, Python, R programming language, might aim to become a data scientist in the future.

❖ **Demographics (Age/Gender/Location):** Interpretations can be made based on demographics For example, candidates within the age range of 25 to 35 years are more active on Instagram/X, Snapchat and with 35 to 45 years are more active on LinkedIn.

❖ **Platforms they Prefer:** Their preferences for knowing about a particular company, career page/social media channels they use, groups they are a part of.

Now that we know about candidate personas and the information needed to create those personas, it is important to understand all the attributes and preferences of the ideal candidates including their job search behaviour, preferred platforms, etc.

This way you can form a communication strategy that resonates with them which wins their attention and offers several advantages including these:

❖ Better Candidate Engagement
❖ Enhanced Candidate Experience
❖ Higher Quality Applicants

❖ Shorter Time to Fill Positions

By adopting persona-driven recruitment marketing, organizations can create a more strategic and impactful approach to talent acquisition, leading to better matches between candidates and available roles.

LET'S SYNTHESIZE

What are the top characteristics of your ideal candidate or a perfect hire? Can you categorize the persona based on those characteristics?

....

....

....

....

....

If you start implementing recruitment marketing strategy without identifying your candidate personas, what difference will it make to the return on investment?

....

....

....

....

....

CONNECTION
AND
ENGAGEMENT

15

A STRONG PERSONAL BRAND

People will remember me by my words, writings, and poems; no matter if they meet me or not because people know us by the way we represent ourselves. People know us the way we wanted them to know us. People know us even better if we know how to let them know us.

From the time I could read, I remember reading poems written by my father. Whenever he used to write a new poem, he would use his pseudonym or 'pen name' somewhere in the poem. When I asked him the reason, he said, "People will remember me by my words, writings and poems; no matter if they meet me or not because people know us by the way we represent ourselves. People know us the way we wanted them to know us. People know us even better if we know how to let them know us." Having a pen name along with his poems helped people understand about his association with those poems every time they read it or shared it with others.

I could understand what he had said that day better when I grew up as a writer myself. We are not only what we think, we are what we write, express, and show and people remember us easily when we keep reminding them of us. This is what is also known as a personal brand these days.

Wondering why I am talking about it here? Simple reason, as a recruiter, your personal brand is just as important as the candidates you are trying to attract.

Having a strong personal brand can be a key factor in attracting the attention of candidates and building long-term relationships with them. Also, if people know you, they establish a connection with you. The more connected you are, the more talent you can attract.

> " THE MORE YOU INTERACT WITH PEOPLE, THE MORE EVENTS YOU ATTEND, THE MORE KNOWLEDGE YOU SHARE, THE MORE IMPACT YOU CREATE FOR YOURSELF AND YOUR COMPANY. "

Why do you need a strong personal brand?

* **Establishes credibility:** Building a strong personal brand can help establish credibility in the industry. By sharing your knowledge and expertise, you can position yourself as a subject matter expert and thought leader in the recruitment industry. This can help you further build strong relationships with candidates, clients, and colleagues.

* **Attracts Talent:** A strong personal brand can help recruiters stand out from the crowd and attract the attention of highly skilled and talented candidates. If you are a well-known recruiter in the industry, your job postings, articles, and updates will generate noticeable pull on social media platforms like LinkedIn, Instagram, Facebook, X, etc.

❖ **Builds a Strong Network:** Networking is an important aspect of all industries, and it is especially necessary when it is the recruitment industry. The more connected you are with industry leaders, academics, hiring managers and prospective hires, the more visibility you get as a recruiter. Networking should not only be limited to social media. The more you interact with people, the more events you attend, the more knowledge you share, the more impact you create for yourself and your company.

❖ **Improves Outcomes:** A strong personal brand helps recruiters enhance their recruitment outcomes. This helps attract higher-quality candidates, improve retention rates, and contributes to a strong employer brand which again helps attract the best and the loop continues.

❖ **Encourages Competition:** It is important for us as recruiters to stay competitive, adapt to new recruiting and attraction trends and technologies, stay active on social media, attend important and relevant events in the industry whenever we get the opportunity and continue to learn and grow.

We have talked about why we need a strong personal brand, but we should also have a checklist to ensure we are moving in the right direction.

❖ **Curate a Dynamic Online Persona:** It is important to maintain an engaging LinkedIn profile, by regularly updating it with insights, endorsements, and thought-provoking content. Keep your profile updated with the latest headshot and work experience. Makeover your LinkedIn Profile or develop a personal website or Facebook Page/Instagram handle/YouTube channel to provide a comprehensive view of your achievements, testimonials, and a convenient way to contact you.

❖ **Define Your Unique Value Proposition:** Once you have a strong professional presence on LinkedIn and other platforms, define the distinct qualities that make you a go-to person as a recruiter, emphasizing your unique skills and approach.

❖ **Elevate Your Voice in the industry:** You need to showcase your expertise by sharing valuable insights, articles, and actively participating in discussions within your community.

❖ **Forge Connections:** Actively network at industry events, join professional and technical groups of talented professionals you might hire from in the future and cultivate relationships with them to expand your reach.

❖ **Stay Informed:** Keep yourself updated with new recruiting and industry trends and technological advancements to remain an informed professional.

❖ **Project Your Success:** Highlight your wins, outcomes and achievements. This establishes your credibility in your network and for the candidates who follow you.

LET'S SYNTHESIZE

Do you think you have been able to establish a strong personal brand for yourself? If yes, what unique value propositions do you carry with yourself?

....

....

....

....

....

If you were to do one thing at a time in terms of establishing your personal brand as a recruiter, what would be your first step?

....

....

....

....

....

16

PREPARING A TALENT POOL
AND NURTURING THE EXISTING DATABASE

Have you ever wondered how our parents managed the grocery requirements of the household by stocking frequently used items like sugar, salt, tea, coffee, rice, pulses, cereals, etc., so that they don't have to go shopping to get those things each time the need arose.

When it comes to applying the same logic to our jobs at recruitment, we tend to move our focus to the demands that already exist. We are always so occupied in working for positions which are currently open that we tend to miss out on the ones which are more likely to come up in future and our fight for finding the best talent always goes on, and we get caught up in a first-come-first-serve demand and supply philosophy.

What if we have a talent pool already in place, and we find them a matching demand instead of supplying matching talent for the demand? What if we start following a reverse methodology? What if we identify a talent pool based on the organization's goals, mission and cultural values, and nurture them by engaging with them and keeping them up to date with new technology and trends the organization is shifting towards so that they are technically and culturally prepared?

Having a talent pool is like having a stock of important things always ready which can help organizations to quickly fill vacancies with suitable candidates, save time and money spent towards recruitment efforts, and ensure that they have a steady supply of skilled employees who can help drive growth and innovation.

For example, if based on the historical data and future hiring forecasting, you already know that you would need software engineers with experience in python and networking, you should have an ongoing pipeline for those candidates. As soon as a new demand arises, you need not start from scratch and do fresh sourcing. All you need is to consider the existing pipeline and connect with them.

There are a few key steps to nurture the existing database and create the new one:

- ❖ **Define the Skills and Competencies You Need:** Just as you stock your home on the basis of the frequency of usage, similarly, the first step in building a talent pool is to identify the skills and competencies that are required for your organization by analyzing the skill set of the current workforce and identifying any gaps that need to be filled.

- ❖ **Develop a Recruitment Strategy:** Once you have identified the skills and competencies that you need, the next step is to develop a recruitment strategy for building the talent pool. This may involve identifying recruitment levers such as job boards, social media, employee referrals, and recruitment agencies.

❖ **Create a Database of Potential Candidates:** As you begin to receive applications and resumes, it is important to create and refresh the database of potential candidates. This may involve having a strong Applicant Tracking System (ATS), Candidate Relationship Management tool (CRM) or a spreadsheet to keep track of candidate information.

❖ **Nurture Your Talent Pool:** It is important to remember that building a talent pool is an ongoing process. Even after you have filled a position, you should continue to nurture your talent pool by staying connected with potential candidates, engaging with them, sharing company news and developments, and providing them with the latest updates.

❖ **Measure ROI of Talent Pipeline:** It is particularly important to measure the effectiveness of your talent pipeline. This may involve keeping track of recruitment metrics such as time-to-hire, cost per hire, retention rates, and candidate experience.

I would like to share different ways of creating a talent pipeline:

❖ **Leverage your CRM Tool:** Once you have identified skills for building a talent pipeline, you should start creating talent communities specific to those skills in your CRM tool.

❖ **Utilize LinkedIn Projects:** If there are certain skills you always hire for, try to maintain your LinkedIn projects.

It provides options to save your search strings, review talent insights within the project based on the search string, add suitable candidates and recommended matches to the pipeline, set search alerts so that any new candidate with similar skills reflects within the project and can be added to the pipeline.

❖ **Refresh Your Existing Database:** Companies that have been hiring for certain positions for a long time have a strong database of suitable candidates. What is missing is that the resumes of the candidates are not always updated. Within a specific time interval, we need to run a database refresh activity to encourage candidates to update their resumes to target them for suitable opportunities.

Creating a talent pool and connecting them with respective talent communities and then nurturing it through CRM tools is an ideal way to ensure that the organization is always ready to hire for upcoming positions based on their historical hiring trend and demand forecasting.

LET'S SYNTHESIZE

What method would you prefer to manage your talent pipeline for the skills you hire the most?

....

....

....

....

....

17

EFFECTIVE COMMUNICATION

Words play an important role in our day-to-day communication. The way we articulate things helps the audience perceive our intentions and decide the response.

Once we source or attract candidates for our requirements, it is also important to find ways to communicate with them and be clear about our message. As a recruiter or sourcer, it is always advisable to have your elevator pitch ready and initiate ways to communicate effectively.

Effective communication with candidates is crucial for several reasons, and it plays an important role in the success of the full recruitment life cycle which starts with attraction and continues till experience. Here are some primary reasons why effective communication is important:

❖ **Enhances Candidate Experience:** Transparent and timely communication creates a positive candidate experience. Even if a candidate is not selected, they are more likely to have a favourable view of the organization if the communication was respectful and informative.

❖ **Builds Trust and Credibility:** Clear communication builds trust between the employer and the candidate. Being transparent about the recruitment process, timelines and expectations brings up credibility and shows respect for the candidate's time and effort.

❖ **Maintains Employer Brand:** Candidates who have positive communication experiences are more likely to share their experiences with others, contributing to a positive employer brand. On the other hand, poor communication can lead to negative reviews and affect the company's image.

❖ **Attracts Top Talent:** A professional and communicative recruitment process appeals to top talent. Candidates are more likely to be interested in working for a company that values clear and respectful communication.

❖ **Engaging with Candidates:** Effective communication is not just about conveying information; it also involves listening to candidates. Engaging in two-way communication helps build relationships and allows candidates to express their concerns and ask questions.

❖ **Improves Decision-Making:** Well-informed candidates are better positioned to make decisions about job offers. Clear communication about the role, expectations and the company's culture enables candidates to make informed choices.

❖ **Compliance:** Effective communication helps ensure compliance with legal and regulatory requirements. Clearly communicating the reasons for selection or non-selection can mitigate potential legal risks associated with discrimination claims.

❖ **Encourages Future Engagement:** Candidates who have positive communication experience, even if not selected, are more likely to consider applying for future openings at the company. This can be valuable for building a talent pool.

Since we have covered why we need to communicate effectively, we also need to know how we communicate and the different channels we could explore to communicate.

It is important to understand that apart from being able to pull insights and attracting talent through various platforms, we also need to reach out to the attracted pool of candidates. This can be done through different ways including InMails and messaging and by tools which help us form more inclusive language.

Creating inclusive and respectful communication is crucial when reaching out to candidates. Here are some tools and extensions that can help ensure your communication is more inclusive and considerate:

❖ **Textio:** Textio is an AI-powered writing platform that suggests inclusive language and helps improve the overall tone of your communication. It highlights potentially biased language and suggests alternative phrasing to create more inclusive messages.

❖ **Grammarly:** Grammarly is a popular writing assistant that offers a tone detector feature. It can help you identify if your writing sounds overly formal, casual or neutral, which can impact how inclusive and approachable your communication feels.

- ❖ **Hemingway Editor:** Hemingway Editor helps simplify your writing and offers suggestions for clearer and more concise language. This can be beneficial for ensuring that your messages are easily understandable and do not inadvertently exclude anyone.

- ❖ **The Gender Decoder for Job Ads (Chrome Extension):** This extension specifically focuses on job advertisements and helps identify gender-coded language that might discourage certain candidates from applying. It suggests ways to neutralize the language to make it more inclusive.

- ❖ **LanguageTool (Chrome Extension):** LanguageTool is a grammar and style checker that can help ensure your communication is not only grammatically correct but also inclusive and respectful.

- ❖ **Microsoft Word:** Microsoft Word now includes features that offer suggestions for using a more inclusive language. It can identify terms that might be considered biased and gives alternatives.

- ❖ **Tone Analyzer Tools:** Various tone analyzer tools, such as IBM Watson's Tone Analyzer, can help you assess the emotional tone of your communication. This can ensure your messages come across as respectful and considerate.

- ❖ **AI-enabled Messaging Tools:** Many platforms like LinkedIn Recruiter, HireEz, etc. have integrated AI messaging to help the recruiters select inclusive and bias-free messages. These messages are also customized in a manner which appears personal and unique to candidates.

These tools and extensions are valuable in terms of crafting communication that is warm, inclusive and respectful to candidates from all backgrounds and identities.

We need to understand when to use which tool. For example, while drafting a job description, Textio can be used at the initial level proactively, whereas while sending InMails/mails or messages to candidates AI tools and features can be used to ensure that the method of communication is appropriate.

If you pull out LinkedIn usage reports, or get a chance to review them, you will notice that different recruiters have different InMail acceptance rates with similar numbers of candidates contacted. People with high InMail acceptance rates put additional efforts into drafting personalized messages for different candidates. Even with AI suggested messages there is a scope to modify and make the mail more personalized and appealing.

When candidates receive more personalized and informed messages, they tend to respond irrespective of their interest for the position.

> **CREATING INCLUSIVE AND RESPECTFUL COMMUNICATION IS CRUCIAL WHEN REACHING OUT TO CANDIDATES.**

LET'S SYNTHESIZE:

What are the top three best practices you follow while communicating with candidates, particularly in sensitive situations like rejections or negotiations?

....

....

....

....

....

CANDIDATE
EXPERIENCE

18

CANDIDATE EXPERIENCE

I enjoy the way the restaurant staff put efforts to bring everything together to let us know what all they have to offer, "The Value Proposition" and after the order we start experiencing the taste, the ambience, the music, the service, and everything which helps us decide to keep visiting the place, "The Customer Experience.

My family and I love travelling to places, and we love to revisit places which provided us with a delightful experience. We love visiting restaurants which offer us customized services, and put efforts to introduce us to their best food choices. We never mind trusting them with their suggestions as we know that they care about us and our choices.

They offer us the value we look for and they offer us the experience we look for. Before trying the food, I enjoy the way the restaurant staff put efforts to bring everything together to let us know what all they have to offer, "The Value Proposition" and after the order we start experiencing the taste, the ambience, the music, the service, and everything which helps us decide to keep visiting the place, "The Customer Experience."

I still remember the way I went through the interview process of my current organization. Even after three years I remember every interview, the interviewer, and the way they engaged with me, asked the right questions, provided all required details about the role and the expectations from the roles. Every interview happened exactly at the scheduled date and time.

Even during the interview process, I already felt like a part of my organization. Not only this, after I received the offer letter, they kept me engaged through different activities. I was introduced to the team I was supposed to work with, I received calls from the HR head and country head to ask if I had any questions or if there was anything they could help me with. They made me feel that I was important, and that they were looking forward to me joining them. My experience was so amazing that I could not even consider thinking of scheduling any other interview. I felt belonged. When I joined them, I was welcomed by the HR and recruitment team through a nice introduction mail which talked about who I was as a person and what I liked and what my hobbies were. Since I own a pet, Duggu (Daschchund Baby), I was very quickly able to connect with people who had pets and we started talking more than work.

Sharing hobbies and interests helps you connect with like-minded people in an organization.

There was a proper induction planned for the initial month and all the meetings with my stakeholders and fellow team members were scheduled in advance.

When I became one of them, I realized this was how they treated every new joiner, and it was fantastic.

Every candidate to a company should be no less than a customer to a restaurant and hence, their experience is equally important since they are the ones who are responsible for the growth of the company and their contribution plays an important part in the projects, business, revenue, and goals of the company.

The candidate experience was, is and will always be an important criterion to measure the success of the recruitment function of any organization. Candidates who carry great experiences during the recruitment process not only become a delighted employee if selected but they also become the brand ambassador of the company. Even candidates who couldn't clear the selection process take away the experience and the company brand with them for the future.

Few factors which any organization must keep in mind for a better candidate experience:

Clear Communication: Communication is key during the interview process. Candidates should be informed about the process, the timeline, and what they can expect at each stage. Providing clear and timely feedback can help candidates feel more comfortable and confident.

Train the Interviewers or Hiring Managers: Ensure that the hiring managers are prepared and trained to conduct interviews. The hiring managers should be well informed about the role and should ask questions that help assess the candidate's fit for not only the position but also for the organization's long-term goal. Many times we rely completely on the recruitment function to be the face of the organization, but we should remember that candidates will be working with the business and hiring managers closely and so hiring managers are equally accountable for providing great experience to candidates during the interview process.

Personalization and Customizations: Personalization is important when it comes to the interview process. Candidates want to feel like they are more than just a profile for the organization. Customize the interview experience to the individual candidate by providing information about the company culture, the team they will be working with, and the specific challenges they will be facing in the role. Every team has its own unique selling points and method of execution. Candidates deserve to know more about the team structure before becoming part of the team.

Value Candidate's Time: Like the employer who manages multiple job applications, candidates are often managing multiple job interviews, so it is important to respect their time. We need to be clear about the length of the interview and stick to the schedule. Always avoid rescheduling or cancelling interviews as much as possible at the last minute unless it is an emergency.

Provide Timely Feedback: Providing feedback after the interview is an essential component of the candidate's experience. Whether the feedback is positive or negative, it is essential to let candidates know how they performed and how they can improve. Providing constructive feedback can help candidates develop and improve their skills, and it shows that you value their time and effort.

Overall, a positive candidate experience is crucial to attract and retain top talent. By providing a clear and personalized interview process, respecting the candidate's time, and providing feedback, organizations can ensure that candidates feel valued and engaged throughout the process.

LET'S SYNTHESIZE

What are some key points for a good candidate experience, and how can recruiters ensure that they are providing a positive experience at each stage?

....

....

....

....

....

What efforts do you individually put in to provide a great candidate experience?

....

....

....

....

....

19

STRUCTURED INTERVIEWING: A GAME CHANGER

Structured interviewing is a systematic and standardized approach to candidate assessment.

We have already talked about various methods to attract the best available candidates for our organization; we also spoke about the importance of candidate experience. Now, let us try to understand the process of taking them through different steps of the interview process.

Earlier, organizations used to follow traditional methods of interviews where shortlisted candidates were assessed based only on the roles and responsibilities and interviewing was completely dependent on the hiring manager and the way they wanted to interview the candidates. Many companies still use this method with no specific format or steps for the interview process.

As the name suggests, structured interviewing is a systematic and standardized approach to candidate assessment. Unlike unstructured or old methods of interviews, which were more likely to create biases and inconsistencies, structured interviews follow a predefined format. This process aims to ensure there is transparency, reliability, fairness and a thorough evaluation of each candidate.

Important Components of Structured Interviewing are:

❖ **Standardized Questions:** As a first step, it is important to create a set of standardized skill- and role-related questions that all candidates would attempt. This will create consistency in the interview process, provide hiring managers with fixed parameters to evaluate candidates and facilitate fair comparisons.

> AN ORGANIZATION PRACTICING STRUCTURED INTERVIEWING CAN ELEVATE THEIR HIRING PROCESS AND GET RID OF BIASES AND INCONSISTENCIES; WHICH IN TURN LEADS TO A GREAT CANDIDATE EXPERIENCE AND STRONG EMPLOYEE VALUE PROPOSITION.

❖ **Scoring Rubrics:** As a next step, the hiring team needs to develop a scoring system or rubric for each question, outlining the criteria through which responses will be evaluated. This provides accuracy in the scoring system.

❖ **Multiple Interviewers:** Once we have the set of questions and scoring rubrics, it is important to involve multiple interviewers to minimize individual biases. Each interviewer can focus on specific skills or competencies or aspects of the candidate's fitment for the role.

❖ **Training for Interviewers:** As an important step, we need to provide inclusive training to all the interviewers to ensure they understand the structured interviewing process, recognize potential biases and adhere to the guidelines of structured interviewing.

Once you have the parameters to plan for the interview, you should be able to scale it at all levels.

There are several advantages of a structured interview process including the major ones mentioned below:

- ❖ **Reduced Bias:** By using a standardized set of questions and evaluation criteria, structured interviewing helps minimize biases related to factors such as age, gender, or cultural background, leading to a fair and inclusive hiring process.

- ❖ **Consistency Across Candidates:** The uniformity in the interview process ensures that each candidate is evaluated based on the same set of criteria. This consistency is crucial for making informed and reasonable hiring decisions.

- ❖ **Improved Candidate Experience:** All candidates appreciate a well-organized, structured and transparent interview process. Structured interviews contribute to a positive candidate experience by providing clear expectations and an equal opportunity for each participant.

Overall, an organization practicing structured interviewing can elevate their hiring process and get rid of biases and inconsistencies; which in turn leads to a great candidate experience and strong employee value proposition.

LET'S SYNTHESIZE

What are the key components of structured interviewing as per you?

....

....

....

....

....

Do you think structured interviewing is important for reducing bias and improving hiring decisions?

....

....

....

....

....

20

WHY SHOULD I JOIN YOU? UNDERSTANDING EMPLOYEE VALUE PROPOSITION

While organizations assess talent based on multiple attributes, what about candidates? They, too, are equally particular about becoming a part of an organization which would offer not only a job but also a second home, culture, dreams, motivation, long-term career, or maybe a retirement plan.

As a recruiter, we always have a question at the back of our mind at the time of hiring – why should we hire this candidate? We want to see the skill fitment, culture fitment, etc. At the same time, it is important for us to understand that the candidate, too, has some questions in mind. Why should they join you? What is there for them? How would they be able to meet their career goals with this organization? What are the benefits? Is this a place where they would like to spend some crucial years of their life?

All of this reminds me of what I wrote about matchmaking where it is important for both the persons to understand what value they are bringing to each other's families and lives and this outlook helps them in decision-making. While organizations assess talent based on multiple attributes, what about candidates? They, too, are equally particular about becoming a part of an organization which would offer not only a job but also a second home, culture, dreams, motivation, long-term career, or maybe a retirement plan.

Therefore, it is important for us to think about the Employee Value Proposition (EVP) that would answer all these questions for the candidate. In simple words, an EVP is the reason why a candidate would choose to join any organization or why an employee would stay in any organization.

An effective EVP can help attract, retain, and engage talented employees. It can also differentiate the organization from its competitors and improve its overall employer brand.

Few key components of an EVP are:

- ❖ **Compensation and Benefits:** This includes the salary, bonuses and other financial rewards that an employee receives for their work, as well as non-financial benefits such as health insurance, retirement plans and paid time off.

- ❖ **Career Development:** This includes opportunities for learning and growth within the organization, such as training programs, mentorship and career advancement.

- ❖ **Work Environment:** This includes the physical and cultural aspects of the workplace, such as office layout, company culture and work-life balance.

- ❖ **Recognition and Appreciation:** This includes the ways in which an organization acknowledges and rewards its employees for their hard work and contributions, such as awards, promotions and public recognition.

❖ **Purpose and Meaning:** This includes the extent to which an organization's mission and values align with an employee's personal beliefs and goals, and the sense of fulfillment and purpose that comes from working towards a shared goal.

To develop an effective EVP, an organization should consider the requirements, aspirations and expectations of its current and potential employees. This can be done through surveys, focus groups and interviews.

Once an EVP has been established, it should be communicated clearly and consistently to all employees, as well as to potential candidates during the recruitment process. This can be done through various channels such as job descriptions, social media and employee testimonials.

An EVP is like a promise that a company makes to its employees. It tells employees what they can expect from the company and what the company expects from them. A good EVP can help a company attract and keep talented employees, stand out from other companies, and make employees happier. By taking care of its employees and understanding what they want, a company can create a strong EVP that will help it succeed in the long term.

LET'S SYNTHESIZE

What value proposition would you like to communicate to your candidates and at what stage would you wish to communicate these to them?

....

....

....

....

....

According to you, what are the top three parameters of an employee value proposition?

....

....

....

....

....

21

HIRE THEM FOR ATTITUDE, TRAIN THEM IN SKILLS

The ability to communicate effectively, listen actively, and understand a customer's needs are all skills that can be developed over time, but having the right attitude and personality traits can make a big difference.

During my childhood, I was always encouraged to play sports and participate in group activities. I was taught that through such activities, we develop an athletic spirit, become more disciplined, learn how to perform as a group, and understand that success does not necessarily belong to an individual but can be achieved by a group of people. I was also taught that losing a game is not a bad thing; when we win, we win but when we lose, we learn.

All these things helped me to develop the right attitude, enabling me to set aside personal preferences and think collectively. Looking back, I can now see the importance of developing the right attitude, as skills can be developed over time.

I have a deep appreciation for the hiring process of companies that prioritize candidates' aptitude and attitude, and rely on their own training systems to develop their skills.

As humans, we have a natural ability to acquire new skills and stay up to date with technology, especially with the ones we regularly use in our daily work. Through consistent practice, we become proficient in these skills, making us more valuable and productive contributors to the workforce.

The phrase 'Hire them for attitude, train them on skills' has become increasingly popular in the business world in recent years. While skills can be taught, it is much harder to change someone's attitude. Therefore, it is better to hire someone who has the right attitude and train them in the required skills.

While hiring new employees, it is important to look for qualities such as enthusiasm, willingness to learn, positive outlook and a strong work ethic. These are all indicators that the candidate has the right mindset to succeed in the workplace.

Once you have hired someone with a good attitude, it is important to invest in their training and development. Provide them with the tools and resources they need to learn new skills and perform their job to the best of their ability. Offer ongoing support and feedback to help them grow and develop in their role.

Remember that training and development are ongoing processes. Even the most skilled and experienced employee can benefit from further training and development. Continuously investing in your employees' growth and development can help them reach their full potential and lead to the success of the organization.

Here are a few examples of situations where hiring candidates for their attitude may be more important than their current skills:

Customer Service: When we plan to hire for customer service roles, some employers may prioritize candidates who have a positive and empathetic attitude over those with extensive technical skills. This is because it is easier to train someone in the specific processes and procedures involved in the job, but it is much harder to teach someone to have a genuine interest and ability to help customers.

Teamwork: In many jobs, teamwork is essential for success. Employers may look for candidates who have a collaborative mindset, a willingness to support others, and a positive attitude towards working in a team environment. These candidates may be more effective at building relationships with colleagues and contributing to a positive workplace culture, even if they do not have all the technical skills needed for the job.

Innovation: In roles that require innovation and creativity, it may be more important to hire candidates who have a positive and curious attitude, are willing to experiment and take risks, and are open to innovative ideas. Technical skills can be developed, but a mindset that encourages innovation and creativity is essential for driving progress and success.

Entry-Level Positions: For entry-level positions, some employers may prioritize candidates who show a strong work ethic, willingness to learn, and positive attitude, even if they don't have much experience in the field. These candidates may be more open to training and development opportunities and more likely to adapt to the company's culture and values.

Leadership Roles: Companies may look for individuals who have a powerful sense of integrity and the ability to inspire and motivate others, even if they do not have experience in a leadership role. The right attitude and personal qualities can be more important than technical expertise, as they lay the foundation for effective leadership.

Sales and Marketing Roles: In these roles, employers look for candidates who have a natural ability to build relationships and connect with others, even if they do not have a lot of experience in this field. The ability to communicate effectively, listen actively and understand a customer's needs are all skills that can be developed over time, but having the right attitude and personality traits can make a significant difference.

"I have learned over the years that, when you have really good people, you don't have to baby them. By expecting them to do great things, you can get them to do great things."

– Steve Jobs

Overall, when hiring for attitude over skills, it is important to look for candidates who demonstrate a positive attitude, strong integrity, willingness to learn new things, belief in teamwork, and a strong work ethic. These are all traits that can be difficult to train but can make a big difference to an employee's success and overall impact on the organization.

LET'S SYNTHESIZE

As a recruiter how would you assess the attitude of the candidate you are interviewing or screening?

....

....

....

....

....

You interviewed two candidates against the role of a project manager. On the scale of 1 to 10, Candidate A has scored 7 in right attitude and 6 in skills and Candidate B has scored 5 in right attitude and 9 in skills, who would you prefer to hire and why?

....

....

....

....

....

22

APPLICANT TRACKING SYSTEM

When I started my recruitment career, my team and I used excel sheets to maintain candidate's data and their details. Our own computers were used as a database for managing resumes and we used to organize folders based on the skills and roles of candidates. We used to call it a resume dump where countless resumes were saved over multiple years. It required a lot of manual work as whenever we used to get a new position, we were asked to review the resumes in our existing database on different folders as the first step. The whole process was time consuming, and it was difficult to track the status of candidates, so the best practice was to manage trackers in excel along with dates to track the status of candidates.

Everyday someone in the team was responsible for consolidating the tracker and sharing it with the entire team. This system was helpful to some extent but there were many drawbacks:

❖ Resumes were not updated.

❖ Searching for the skills and projects of candidates was not easy.

❖ Bulk action was not possible while we maintained excel and resume dumps.

❖ The only way to communicate with candidates was to merge mail or reach candidates through the mailbox.

❖ It was difficult to track and update all the activities of candidates.

❖ Engaging with candidates and sharing feedback with them required additional effort.

We faced multiple issues till we onboarded an Applicant Tracking System (ATS) to our recruiting process. As the name implies, ATS is an internal system very crucial to the recruitment process. It facilitates the tracking of all stages in the recruitment cycle for each applicant. Once a job is posted externally or internally, candidates apply, becoming a part of the ATS. Every action on their application is recorded.

Organizations use different ATSs with varying terminologies, however, the core process remains consistent:

❖ **Screening:** Resumes are screened by the sourcer/recruiter once the profiles are sourced or attracted to ATS.

❖ **Hiring Manager Review:**
   + Profile is shared with hiring manager for their feedback and review
   + If the profile is rejected, the candidate is notified via email with feedback.
   + If the profile is shortlisted, the recruiter proceeds with the next steps.

❖ **Phone Screening:**

✦ Recruiters schedule a screening call with candidates with a set of screening questions.

✦ Phone screening feedback is captured in the system and shared with hiring managers

❖ **Interviews:**

✦ Interviews are scheduled if the candidates qualify at the screening stage.

✦ Candidates are informed with feedback if they are selected or rejected for the next round of interviews.

✦ After technical interviews, a final HR round is arranged to discuss compensation, role and location.

❖ **Offer Management:**

✦ Once the HR round is completed with candidate expectations of the role and compensation discussed, the offer approval process begins with HR and business leaders who own the hiring positions.

✦ If salary expectations exceed the budget, offers may not be approved.

✦ Once the offer is approved, the recruitment team initiates documentation, collects necessary documents, and starts background verification.

✦ After successful background verification, the offer is extended to the candidate with the specified joining date.

❖ **Onboarding**

✦ The candidate moves to the onboarding stage after accepting the offer and completing all documentation.

+ The onboarding team manages the candidate's onboarding on the date of joining.
+ Recruiters mark the candidate as hired in the ATS and the recruitment life cycle of a candidate gets completed.

Having a strong ATS is essential for any organization to make the recruitment process flawless.

Here are a few reasons:

Increases Efficiency and Saves Time: Many ATSs can automate various stages of the hiring process, such as resume screening, application tracking and interview scheduling. This significantly reduces the time spent on manual steps and allows recruiters to focus more on personalized steps including candidate engagement, offer negotiation, etc.

Acts as a CRM Tool: All applicant tracking systems provide a centralized database for managing candidate information. Recruiters can easily access and track candidate details, review their previous interviews and feedback, and assess their profiles against all job postings. The profiles can even be considered for new positions. Few ATSs provide separate CRM and enable recruiters or sourcers to apply filters and search candidate profiles based on the job description. Effective search criteria makes CRM tools the go-to platform for sourcing candidates as those candidates are more likely to be more aware of the brand.

Communication with Candidates through ATS or CRM: Most ATS and CRM tools provide communication methods among hiring team members. Candidates are informed in real time about every activity performed against their profile starting from screening to onboarding.

ATSs have integrated features like automated email responses and status notifications, which provides a facility to ensure candidates are kept informed about their application status during the entire hiring process. This contributes to a positive candidate experience, even for those who may not be selected.

Compliance and Standardization: Through ATS, recruitment processes adhere to legal and regulatory requirements. It provides a standardized framework for documentation, ensuring consistency in hiring practices and reducing the risk of non-compliance.

Integration with other HR Systems: Many ATS platforms are easily able to integrate with other Human Resources Information Systems (HRIS).

Talent Pool Building through CRM: ATS CRM enables the creation of talent pools by storing candidate information for future roles. Recruiters can proactively tap into this talent pool, reducing the time needed to fill for future positions.

To summarize, ATS and CRM are two sides of one coin, both have equal importance, and both perform specific functions. ATS has a major role to play when it comes to working on active positions and perform activity on candidates who have applied to active positions and move the candidates to different steps of the recruiting process whereas CRM is considered as a more proactive approach of recruiting where the recruiters work on pipelining for future roles and engage with passive candidates and nurture relationships with them.

Workday Recruiting, iCIMS Talent Cloud, Jobvite, SmartRecruiters and SAP Success Factor are a few examples of widely recognized Applicant Tracking Systems.

LET'S SYNTHESIZE

List the names of different applicant tracking systems you have used as a recruiter or experienced as a candidate. Which one was the most effective?

....

....

....

....

....

23

REVIEW PLATFORMS FOR STRONG EMPLOYER BRAND

Do you watch movies or web series? If yes, what makes you decide which movie to watch? Word of mouth? Movie Reviews? Influencers? I am sure, whether you go with the face value of the actors, or you go by your research, most of you have some set parameters to decide before going for a movie. Though some people may take a risk, when it comes to movies, my husband and I do not miss even a single opportunity to watch a good movie. However, the term 'good' in the context of movies depends on several factors which apply to the whole range of merely satisfactory to truly exceptional.

Like many of you, prior to booking our tickets, we look at reviews provided by fellow moviegoers, relying on their perspectives and the overall ratings to guide our decision. Whether it is a four or five or an eight on ten, these evaluations give us a sense of confidence in our choices, reassuring us that we are making well-informed selections.

Similarly, in the world of recruitment, job seekers have been quick to adopt this trend, researching proactively about employers online before applying for their job or accepting the offers. Hence the review platforms hold significant power in setting up expectations and forming perceptions for any organization's employer brand, as these platforms provide important feedback for candidates evaluating their potential workplaces.

To explain more, these review platforms provide an interface for current and former employees to share their experiences openly and anonymously. The reviews available on these platforms offer transparency and authenticity that is not possible otherwise through an organization's employer branding efforts.

Transparency and authenticity is the foundation for any strong employer brand, and all the reviews by employees or candidates which are often honest and candid help convey an authentic interpretation of the mission, vision, value, and work culture of the organization.

GLASSDOOR

Let us dive deeper into how Glassdoor, as one of the prominent review platforms, contributes to building a strong employer brand.

Sharing some of the important features which Glassdoor provides to establish itself as one of the few strong go-to platforms for candidates researching employer brands.

- ❖ **Overall Company Ratings:** As a candidate while researching your prospective employers, you can see the overall ratings of any employer listed on Glassdoor. The ratings range from one to five, five being the highest.

Many candidates drop the idea of joining an organization if they have low Glassdoor ratings and on the other hand, when they see higher ratings or above average ratings, they continue to do further research on the brand.

❖ **Employee Reviews and Ratings:** Glassdoor provides an anonymous rating mechanism for current and former employees, and external candidates who have experienced any kind of engagement with the employer based on the categories below:
  + Culture and Values
  + Diversity and Inclusion
  + Career Opportunities
  + Work/Life Balance
  + Senior Management
  + Compensation and Benefits

These reviews provide job seekers with a clear view of an organization's work environment, helping them make informed decisions.

❖ **Jobs:** Glassdoor provides a separate section to employers where all the open jobs are listed. These jobs directly get linked to the career page of the company, so they reflect in real time. Any candidate researching the organization can also review the jobs and can directly apply via Glassdoor. This is why Glassdoor is also considered as an important platform for attracting candidates who are informed decision makers and are serious about the company and the roles they are applying for.

❖ **Salaries:** Another important section in Glassdoor is the salary section. Employees can share their salary information, including base pay and bonuses, which provides job seekers with a clear picture of compensation. It helps them set right expectations from the very start.

❖ **Interviews:** This is one of the most important sections for candidates who are visiting Glassdoor to not only be aware about the brand they are applying to but also want to prepare and learn about the interview process. Job seekers can refer to various interview reviews based on the skills they have and can prepare themselves accordingly.

❖ **Employer Brand Management:** Glassdoor provides tools for organizations to actively manage their employer brand. Companies can add details, updates, news, respond to reviews, and engage with current and potential employees. This engagement allows organizations to demonstrate their commitment to addressing concerns and fosters a positive work environment.

❖ **Benefits:** This section provides a consolidated view of benefits given by the organization and the ratings associated with those benefits. This helps job seekers to assess the value proposition the organization is going to offer to the employee.

❖ **Awards and Recognitions:** Glassdoor annually publishes its 'Best Places to Work' list based on employee reviews and ratings. Earning a spot on this list is a prestigious accolade that can significantly enhance an organization's employer brand.

Now when you know that candidates look at your brand before making any decision to join or apply to job postings, there are strong reasons why you should consider these review platforms as an integral part of recruitment.

Why should an employer encourage these platforms?

❖ **Empowering and Encouraging Employees:** When employees are encouraged to share their thoughts and experiences on review platforms, it empowers them and creates a sense of belonging within the organization. This leads to employees feeling more engaged and acts like a strong advocate for the organization.

❖ **Perception Management:** At times, job seekers rely on what they have heard about the organization over the years and base their perception off of it. This could be the feedback they have heard from their friends or family members or the organization's social media presence and marketing. A strong presence on review platforms like Glassdoor helps manage or validate those perceptions. When we hear about a company through word of mouth or through ads, we may not get the entire picture. However, when there is data to support the perception that has been built by the employer, a candidate is reassured about their choice.

❖ **Employer Brand Validation:** Organizations use employee advocacy on their social media channels like Facebook/Instagram and networking platforms like

LinkedIn. When employees share their own stories on their social channels, it makes an impact on the job seekers and when they further validate similar feedback from review platforms like Glassdoor/Indeed they become assured.

❖ **Continuous Improvement:** Based on employees'/ former employees' feedback, employers can review these analytically and act accordingly.

Like the internal surveys that seek feedback from current employees, work on the strengths and weaknesses, and plan future strategy, review platforms help organizations seek feedback from candidates who are not a part of the system but have engaged with the organization during the interview process or have been associated with the company previously.

These platforms give the candidate broader aspects of all important parameters which are important for any employer to be an established brand.

LET'S SYNTHESIZE

If you were a candidate willing to apply for a company, how would you do your primary research?

....

....

....

....

....

What parameters are important for an employer to attract the best candidates? What parameters are important to you as a candidate?

....

....

....

....

....

24

ALEXA! PLEASE FIND ME A SUPERMAN!

Few call AI a curse as it is certainly making humans dependent, but I call it an opportunity to focus only on innovations and creativity and leave the things which are already being done earlier as we have Alexas, Siris and Chat GPT kind of assistants to take care of our ask for regular things.

The world is slowly getting used to Alexa and Siri. At work, AI based robotics assistants have made life much easier. It wasn't too long ago that robots were considered a thing of the future.

Now, you just have to command, and it's done. The future is here. Few call AI a curse. They claim that AI will make humans dependent, but I see it as an opportunity to focus on innovation and creativity and leave repetitive and monotonous tasks to AI assistants like Alexa, Siri, ChatGPT, etc.

Soon, there will be a time when you would just need to publish your requirement on one platform and it will be available on all the platforms. Similarly, a job seeker would only need to upload their updated resume and they would automatically get the list of matching jobs on their profile page. In times like these, job descriptions and candidate profiles will need to be extremely accurate and precise for relevant results to show up. If you write accurate job descriptions, everything else can be taken care of by AI based tools.

With smartphones acting like spies, sometimes I wonder how the things I think about are right in front of me as an advertisement on my smartphone. We are already in an era when you can expect jobs matching your profile to be right in front of you, just a click away. What we need is more accuracy and relevance.

In my previous organization, I used an AI tool for screening resumes. Instead of recruiters sitting back and screening more than five hundred applications against a job posting, the AI based screening and scoring tool screened the profiles of candidates and even provided the relevance score of candidates in the form of percentage.

Recruiters only needed to update accurate job descriptions which should have specific skills required from any candidate's profile. The tool would screen the resumes based on the skills and requirements on the job descriptions. The closer the resume was to the job descriptions, the better the score.

Over a period, I realized that AI tools were learning from us and changing the scoring method accordingly. The best part of smart and efficient AI tools is that they not only perform tasks on the basis of predefined algorithms but also learn from human interactions. So, if as a user, recruiters select candidates with high scores, AI understands the trend.

On the other hand, if the tool analyzes that the score does not create any difference in the selection ratio, it will change the scoring benchmarks. We as human beings think that there is a science behind all the tools and technology, but there is also an art behind these tools. They learn and listen to you and the more you interact with them, engage with them, the more they reciprocate.

When I review my entire day at work, I can see how much my team and I utilize AI tools for increasing the efficiency of our work.

It is worth sharing a list of the few AI tools many of the recruitment professionals use in their day-to-day job. We have already covered a few of them in previous chapters.

1. **Textio:** It analyzes job descriptions for language and inclusivity which further helps in attracting a diverse pool of candidates.
2. **HireVue:** HireVue is a video interviewing technology vendor that allows recruiters and hiring managers to screen candidates and conduct live interviews over the internet.
3. **Entelo:** Entelo leverages AI to identify and engage passive candidates by analyzing online data and social media activity.
4. **Ideal:** This tool uses AI to screen and shortlist new applicants and engages with the candidates to gather more information.
5. **LinkedIn Talent Solutions:** LinkedIn Talent Solutions integrates AI to help recruiters find suitable candidates, analyze talent trends, and provide insights for talent acquisition strategies.
6. **XOR.ai:** XOR.ai recruiter attracts, pre-screens and schedules the candidates on behalf of recruiters who

can further take the process ahead for hiring.

Apart from these tools, **LinkedIn Recruiter** and **HireEz** are used for sourcing candidates and their updated version of candidate engagement through in-mails/emails has leveraged AI to create templates/communication based on the candidate's profiles and requirements.

Very soon, resume searching will happen through AI enabled platforms. Based on your search pattern, AI will suggest the next searches.

We are already in an era where we have an Alexa at home to help manage our electronic appliances, Siri to help manage our smartphones, ChatGPT to answer all your questions and generate content.

In the world of recruitment, I am hoping for a day when I say, "Alexa, can you find me a superman to perform my job?" And it will help me reach the best possible talent.

LET'S SYNTHESIZE

How are you utilizing AI in your day-to-day job?

....

....

....

....

....

What are some potential benefits and challenges of using AI in recruitment?

....

....

....

....

....

As per you, how can recruiters use AI tools like chatbots and resume screening software effectively while still providing a positive candidate experience?

....

....

....

....

....

25

CANDIDATE OFFER AND ONBOARDING

Every chapter so far has been about recruiting concluding with hiring a suitable employee for the organization. The entire recruitment life-cycle is carried out with the intention of onboarding the candidate.

In the process of acquiring talent, it is important to effectively manage candidate offers and offer seamless onboarding. Once you have the shortlisted candidates who have cleared all interview rounds through a structured interview process, you need to ensure they are accurately mapped to the open positions. Before you roll out the offer, you need to ensure they are being evaluated on the following criteria:

❖ **Skill Alignment:** As a first step, ensure that the shortlisted candidate has the skills and competencies needed for the role.

❖ **Cultural Fit:** Secondly, assess the candidate for cultural fitment. This can be done by learning how well the candidate aligns with the company's values and work culture.

❖ **Compensation and Benefits:** As a next step, find the compensation fitment, including salary, bonuses and benefits. Make sure it aligns with industry standards and meets the candidate's expectations.

❖ **Reference Checks:** Once the skill, cultural and compensation fitment has been taken into consideration, conduct thorough reference checks to confirm professional background and specified experience of the candidates.

❖ **Documentation:** Request candidates to provide their personal identification details, experience letters of previous employment, salary slips, address proof, etc., to be eligible for receiving the offer letter.

Once the candidate has completed the documentation and the offer has been rolled out, the candidate is required to give a formal acceptance to the letter. This way the candidate is considered as onboarded and the onboarding team follows an engagement plan to keep the candidate engaged before they join on the agreed upon joining date.

OFFER-TO-JOINING CONVERSION

Offer-to-joining conversion shows the success rate of the candidate selected vs candidate joined. For example, if ten selected candidates were offered jobs and seven candidates joined and three declined the offer due to various reasons, the offer to join conversion is seventy per cent and the offer-to-join ratio is 10:7.

There are numerous factors which lead to a better conversion:

❖ **Treat Every Candidate Differently:** Initiate the conversation with the candidates based on their interests and aspirations. A unified approach may not work for all candidates, so personalize your approach and create a sense of belonging within candidates to ensure they feel they are already a part of the organization.

❖ **Communicate Effectively and with Clarity:** Engage with candidates and make yourself available to address all their queries till they are on board and join the organization. They also need to be updated about the compensation range, date of joining, etc., and should agree to that before the offer is rolled out.

❖ **Negotiate but be Flexible:** Offer negotiation is one of the most important aspects of any offer process. As a recruiter, you have an important role to play on behalf of your organization during the negotiation as you need to take care of the cost per hire and salary range. However, you are also responsible for a good candidate experience so be flexible on certain areas like location, date of joining, joining bonus, etc., which can create a great candidate experience and increase the likelihood of successful onboarding.

LET'S SYNTHESIZE

What key factors would you like to implement or see in an onboarding process for a smooth new hiring?

....

....

....

....

....

What are the biggest challenges candidates face in general during the current onboarding process of your organization?

....

....

....

....

....

26
RECRUITMENT METRICS

We have learned about ranking systems at school. We have also experienced the importance of performance and results. Our entire education system relies on assigning scores against performance. Recruitment metrics are not any different.

We have been taught since childhood through schools about our ranking systems. We have also learned from our parents the importance of performance and results. During our entire education system, we have always given scores against our performances in all the subjects we studied. Recruitment metrics are nothing different from that.

Metrics is a way of measuring the performance of parameters which are comparable or can set some benchmark to initiate comparison.

Recruitment metrics are measuring tools that companies use to understand how well they are doing in the process of hiring new employees. They help companies keep track of their progress and help improve the process.

Few important recruitment metrics are mentioned as under:

Time-to-Fill: Time-to-Fill helps calculate the duration taken for a job to get filled by calculating the number of days taken from the date the job vacancy was created to the date the vacancy was filled.

For instance, a company has a job opening for a senior software developer. They start the recruitment process on 1 March, and it takes them 45 days to find the right candidate and have them start the job on 15 April. So, the time-to-fill for this position is 45 days.

Cost-per-Hire: The cost involved in recruiting and hiring one candidate, which includes attraction, job platforms cost, marketing, interview, travel cost, etc., is known as cost-per-hire.

There is an easy formula to calculate cost per hire.

$$\text{CPH} = \frac{\text{Internal Recruiting cost} + \text{External recruiting cost}}{\text{Total number of hires}}$$

Time is money. I have noticed that the more time you take to hire a candidate, the more cost gets involved in hiring.

Quality of Hire: Through this metric, the quality of people hired is measured by observing their performance and the results they bring to the business. It helps you figure out if your hiring process is bringing in the right people.

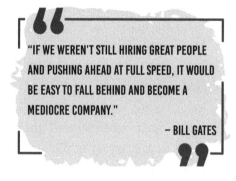

"IF WE WEREN'T STILL HIRING GREAT PEOPLE AND PUSHING AHEAD AT FULL SPEED, IT WOULD BE EASY TO FALL BEHIND AND BECOME A MEDIOCRE COMPANY."

– BILL GATES

Source of Hire: We have already covered different platforms we can access to attract candidates or reach out to candidates.

Source of hire tells about the original platform through which candidates have applied on the job posting or have been sourced from.

It is important for every company to measure the actual source of hires as this helps in deciding which platform attracts more candidates. For example, Company ABC has closed 560 positions at the end of financial year and their source of hires was recorded as follows:

LinkedIn:	40%
Glassdoor:	20%
Careers Page:	20%
Others:	20%

Offer to Joining Conversion: We have already covered a little about it in the previous chapter. This metric helps in analyzing the effectiveness of candidate engagement and candidate conversion. Out of the total number of candidates who were selected and offered, there would be a certain number of candidates who would join the organization, and few may decline the offers due to various reasons.

Offer to joining conversion can be measured by the following simple formula:

$$\text{OFFER TO JOINING CONVERSION} = \frac{\text{Total Number of Hires + Total Offers Declined}}{\text{Total Offers Generated}}$$

Most companies also keep track of different reasons for declining the offers. This helps them to work on improving the conversion by focusing on areas which lead to highest offer decline.

Retention Rate: After hiring, it is important to see how long employees stay with the company. A high retention rate means people are happy and likely to stay for a while. For example, if after two years, ninety per cent of the marketing managers hired are still with the company. This means the company has a ninety per cent retention rate for this role.

Applicant-to-Interview Ratio: This ratio helps you understand how many job applicants make it to the interview stage. It can show if your job descriptions are attracting the right people. Let us say the company received one hundred job applications for the marketing manager role, and after reviewing them, they selected twenty candidates for interviews. So, the Applicant-to-Interview ratio is 100:20, which simplifies to 5:1.

Diversity Metrics: Most of the companies now track the diversity of hires which helps them improve on the efforts of attracting diverse candidates and build a more inclusive workplace.

These recruiting metrics help companies follow a data-driven approach, enhance the recruitment process and plan hiring numbers to achieve the goal of the organization.

LET'S SYNTHESIZE

What are the key metrics which, if tracked effectively, can lead to an effective recruitment function?

....

....

....

....

....

What difference will it make to a recruitment as a function if we do not track recruitment metrics?

....

....

....

....

....

27
A STICKY NOTE

Write your book, write your future. The goals!

In order to achieve your goals and to live your dreams it is important to think about your dreams. Everything we want to achieve requires additional effort and a consistent approach.

You may not be able to get what you want in just a year or two; sometimes it requires years to land at the place where you wanted to be. I have a theory that it takes a minimum of three years of consistent efforts to live your dreams. You must set a target and work towards it continuously without diversion.

In my case, everything I achieved so far happened because I thought about it and then worked in that direction to achieve it. Be it my first corporate job, my first job in recruitment after my journey as an entrepreneur, my aspiration of working in a world class culture in a global organization or my aspiration of authoring a book which can inspire several recruiters and people who wanted to understand recruitment as a function.

I decided to write this book three years back as a New Year resolution and then I kept writing in bits as and when I got some time during weekends or holidays.

In the last two months, while I was struggling to finalize the manuscript and conclude it, I saw a sticky note on my laptop with a beautiful message: 'Write your book, write your future. The goals!'

This sticky note was written by my daughter, who always tells me to spend more time with her. This note from her acted like a motivator as she was willing to sacrifice her 'Mom and Me time' to help me live my dream. It meant giving preference to my book and dedicating my long weekends and holidays to completing this book.

Every time I completed a chapter, I would be inspired by recruiters who worked towards fulfilling dreams of many aspiring professionals who wanted to land their dream job in a dream company. I am so glad that I was able to complete this book for those recruitment professionals and I know that this is just the beginning.

This book is also meant to guide professionals who took a break in their careers because of personal reasons and are planning a comeback. This profession will happily welcome them because recruitment requires an attitude to give the best.

"I am convinced that nothing we do is more important than hiring and developing people. At the end of the day, you bet on people and just not on strategies."

– Lawrence Bossidy
Chairman and CEO, Honeywell International Inc.

28
SELF-LEARNING CHECKLIST

For every audience or reader, it is important to be able to answer the question *'What's in it for me?'* when they pick up something to read or watch. If you know the purpose of completing a course, gaining a degree or certification, or reading a book, you are in the best situation to experience the outcomes and implement the learnings.

It is important for me to take you through a checklist which can help you check whether you achieved your objective behind reading this book. I would like you to review this checklist and analyze your own takeaways. Recruitment is a vast topic, and it includes several sub-topics which can be considered as separate topics for publishing. However, it is important to get the basics aligned and clear. If you are able to mark 'yes' as an answer for at least seventy per cent of the questions below, I would believe that I did some justice to the purpose of writing this book.

Here is your checklist:

	YES	NO	MAYBE
Have I gained an understanding of the basic principles and processes of recruitment?	YES	NO	MAYBE
Can I identify the common challenges faced by recruiters and how to address them?	YES	NO	MAYBE
Have I learned about the different sourcing and attraction strategies used in recruitment?	YES	NO	MAYBE
Can I use Boolean search effectively to find the right candidates?	YES	NO	MAYBE
Do I understand the importance of hiring for diversity and strategies to build a diverse candidate pool?	YES	NO	MAYBE
Have I gained insight into best practices for creating and maintaining a talent pipeline?	YES	NO	MAYBE
Can I communicate effectively with candidates at each stage of the hiring process?	YES	NO	MAYBE
Have I learned about the benefits of structured interviewing?	YES	NO	MAYBE
Do I understand the reason for having a compelling employee value proposition to attract and retain top talent?	YES	NO	MAYBE
Do I know how to use metrics to measure the success of recruitment efforts and inform hiring strategies?	YES	NO	MAYBE

Do I understand the importance of insights into recruitment marketing, review platforms, and other approaches to building a strong employer brand?	YES	NO	MAYBE
Am I familiar with AI tools and technologies used in recruitment?	YES	NO	MAYBE
Have I learned the basics of the offer and onboarding process?	YES	NO	MAYBE
Can I identify my strengths and areas of improvement in recruitment and hiring processes?	YES	NO	MAYBE
Have I gained valuable insights that can help me enhance my recruitment skills and knowledge?	YES	NO	MAYBE
MY SCORE:			

Milton Keynes UK
Ingram Content Group UK Ltd.
UKHW021834130624
444169UK00001B/2